The Radio &Television Commercial

Third Edition

Albert C. Book   Norman D. Cary   Stanley I. Tannenbaum

REVISED BY FRANK R. BRADY

Printed on recyclable paper

NTC Business Books
a division of *NTC Publishing Group* • Lincolnwood, Illinois USA

2/97

#32552178

Library of Congress Cataloging-in-Publication Data

The radio & television commercial / Albert C. Book... [et al.]. —
    3rd ed.
            p.   cm.
        Rev. ed. of: Radio & television commercial / Albert C. Book,
    Norman D. Cary, Stanley I. Tannenbaum. 2nd ed. c1984.
        Includes bibliographical references (p.).
        ISBN 0-8442-3013-8 (pbk.)
        1. Broadcast advertising—United States.   2. Radio advertising—
    United States.   3. Television advertising—United States.
    I. Book, Albert C.   II. Book, Albert C.   Radio & television
    commercial
    HF6146.B74B66   1995
    659.14—dc20   95-11307
                                                     CIP

Published by NTC Business Books, a division of NTC Publishing Group
4255 West Touhy Avenue
Lincolnwood (Chicago), Illinois 60646-1975, U.S.A.

6 7 8 9 ML 0 9 8 7 6 5 4 3 2 1

Contents

Preface

This book teaches the art of creating effective radio and television advertising by combining science with creativity. It is intended to guide the individual who may be preparing for a career in advertising, marketing, or an associated area. The principles of effective TV and radio advertising are examined using analyses of current radio and TV commercials, and practical guides toward producing and judging well-designed sales messages are given.

The information provided will also serve as a background for the copywriter, art director, producer, account executive, or ad manager who wishes to produce well-designed, well-written, and professionally produced commercials.

Your goal may be to help create commercials for an ad agency, or to judge them as a client. Right now, you have ideas. This book will help you to develop a sense of form and craftsmanship so that you can incorporate your ideas into commercials that will be noticed and acted on.

Since the last edition of this book, three things about broadcast advertising have changed tremendously, while the most important thing has not changed at all.

The *appearance* of TV commercials has changed over the past decade. It all started with MTV. Then came "MTV programs" such as *Miami Vice.* "MTV commercials" were not far behind. They are more visual, more quickly paced, use more camera movement, and often combine multiple looks, such as black and white with color, or stills with quick cuts.

The *technology* of TV commercials has also changed. Ten years ago, commercials were shot on film and usually edited on videotape. Today, commercials may be shot on film or videotape. They are almost always edited on a computer. Radio commercials may be created on digital audio tape (DAT), which eliminates tape hiss and allows for an unlimited number of dupes that sound exactly like the original. Technology has also created new special effects and made the old ones more affordable as well as easier to do.

The *form* of TV commercials is the third thing that has changed. Today there are many more forms than a decade ago. One-minute and two-minute direct response commercials are a staple, as are 30-minute informercials. Some cable networks are devoted to shopping. And we are on the verge of interactive shopping on television.

And what is the one thing—the most important thing—that has not changed? It is the objective of a radio or TV commercial: to change the attitude and behaviors of people in order to sell a product or service.

While appearance, technology, and form change, people do not. They still have the same hopes and fears, wants and wishes. So, although newer examples of commercials are used, the essence of the book remains the same. It shows how to sell to people on radio and TV.

There are a few more things that never seem to change. Every writer must have help. I am indebted to many individuals who work for the

v

companies—clients and advertising agencies—whose work appears in this book. A special thanks to Bert Berdis for the radio spots. Thanks, too, to my editor, Rich Hagle, for giving me this opportunity. Finally, one more thing that never changes is that every writer needs someone who is willing to read a manuscript again and again, always with a fresh eye, editing, polishing, and making suggestions large and small. For me, that someone is my wife and best friend, Jennie. To her, I dedicate the Third Edition of *The Radio & Television Commercial.*

F.R.B.

Section One

Broadcast Advertising

1

Creating the Commercial

It is a miracle or the devil's work, depending on your point of view. Voices—living, breathing human voices—traveling hundreds or thousands of miles through the air, unseen and unfelt, until they arrive where we are. And wherever we are: at our homes, in our cars, on the beach, jogging, roller blading, even swimming. They are all about, these voices, coaxing, charming, and convincing us to buy, buy, buy.

What could be a more effective selling tool than radio? Only this, adding moving pictures to the sounds. In a word: television. While it lacks radio's ubiquity (you cannot watch TV while you are driving) it more than makes up for it in efficacy. "Seeing is believing," and TV capitalizes with demonstrations, testimonials, and celebrity endorsers galore.

Certainly newspapers, magazines, billboards, direct mail, and other media are effective, but they are not "alive." They are passive. They do not come to us, we must come to them. We must participate and pay attention. We do not have to do any of that with radio and TV. We only have to stay awake—and not change the channel—to be sold.

Media that Cannot Be Ignored

Although radio and television have the opportunity to appeal to potential consumers in a powerful way, they also have a unique disadvantage.

A newspaper or magazine ad can be ignored. But television and radio commercials interrupt programming. They displace everything else in the medium. They force themselves on the consciousness. And they must run out their time span before the audience can return its attention to other contents of the medium. Of course, the audience can stop watching or listening. But changing channels puts one in danger of missing the return of the programming. So the audience is more or less captive.

Another difference with television is that it is multi-use. Families watch it together and children watch it by themselves. Magazines and newspapers can be put away; the tube cannot. The government, broadcasters, and industry trade groups recognize the power of television by the prohibitions they place on it. For example, cigarettes have not been advertised on the air since 1971, while hard liquor has never been advertised. Beer and wine can be advertised, but not consumed in a commercial. The government promotes the use of condoms but does not allow them to be advertised on TV.

Whether or not you agree with these and other restrictions, the point is that the radio and television audience can be more easily attracted and more easily offended. No wonder, then, that the public's responses to radio and television commercials are more vocal and more varied than they are to print advertisements.

Most listeners and viewers accept the fact that commercials are the price they must pay for "free" television and radio programming, but many express negative opinions of broadcast ads. According to a study by Elmo Roper and Associates, although the public's attitude toward TV commercials in particular is more favorable than hostile, the number of people who actively dislike them is substantial.

Why Commercials Fail

In spite of the criticism, radio and television dominate the advertising media. Spots that are decried as irritating and obtrusive often succeed where success counts most—not in winning prizes or in garnering praise for being responsive to consumer criticism, but in selling products. The fact is, the objective of a commercial is to get the prospect to stop, look, listen—and act. And radio and TV spots must be judged, at least by the advertisers who pay for them, on the basis of that criterion alone.

Why, although the effectiveness of radio and television advertising have been amply demonstrated, do some commercials not succeed? Why do many commercials fail to attract and intrigue the listener or viewer and end up either ignored or forgotten? That is, why do they fail to sell? Of course, there are many answers to this questions, but three keep recurring in research. First, many advertising people take for granted that the name of the product or service will be remembered, even though experts have insisted that almost two-thirds of all commercials do not register the name. Second, the construction of many commercials is haphazard to the point of weakness. And third, many TV and radio spots are imitative, even trite. These practices show a costly disregard for the viewer or listener. They insult his or her taste and intelligence. And they therefore result in resentment or generate apathy.

It is impossible to calculate the vast number of radio and television commercials produced in the United States each year. Because radio listening and TV viewing norms vary, it is also very difficult to estimate how many of these commercials are actually seen and heard. But it has been suggested that a young adult might hear 2,500 radio spots and view about 1,000 TV spots each month. For the reasons given above, only a handful of these spots can be considered outstanding selling vehicles. Fewer win awards.

The combined skills of creative people in radio and television advertising are manifested in the award winners of a number of regional and national competitions. The Clio, Echo, Effie, or One Show awards recognize the industry's finest work. Yet, as many advertising professionals claim, awards are not everything. Much of the judging, they say, concentrates on innovative techniques and/or entertaining approaches, rather than on sales effectiveness. This point is well taken. Some commercials, although award winners in competition, have been abject failures in producing sales. Other commercials, not even considered for an award, have led to dramatic upswings in sales curves.

The Importance of Creativity

Creativity is the key ingredient in any successful commercial. But the word is so often used and misused that it is important to determine exactly what it means in order to find out how it applies to advertising.

Creativity can be defined as "different and better." It may help to think of music. How many rock groups sound the same? To stand out, a band must develop its own style; it must be different. But that is not enough. People must like the new sound—it must be better.

It is difficult to be different and better. That is why so much advertising is not particularly creative. But creativity increases efficiency. A different and better ad will attract more people at a lower cost. So creativity should always be a goal of advertising.

Where do different and better ideas come from? Psychologists from William James on have explored the question. Dr. Gary Steiner narrowed the search to commercials. "Every creative idea," he said, "is initially a departure from present ways of doing things." Writers depart from an accepted, workable base because times change, attitudes change, taste and fashions change. And these things change all the more quickly in a society that has a high degree of mobility and a vast quantity of communications. Each change brings with it a new problem or set of problems. So, in the business of marketing and selling, in the use of advertising, new solutions must be found to new problems. And this demands thinking in new ways and combinations."

Dr. Steiner defines creativity as "the ability to produce and implement new and better solutions to any kind of a problem—to the writing of the copy, to the problem of deciding where and when to advertise, to the problem of how to organize a company." Copywriters' and art directors' abilities are always challenged to "produce and implement new and better solutions"— especially when they are pressured by time, budget, and competitive limitations.

While poets create to enlighten and composers to entertain, advertising writers create to change minds and alter buying decisions. This function of creativity should be kept constantly in mind.

David Ogilvy called it "the big idea." Leo Burnett said it was "the inherent drama of the product." But William Bernbach may have best summed it up when he reported on the planning of an important campaign: "We had neither the time nor the money to impress our message through sheer weight and repetition. We had to call in our ally—creativity. We had to startle people into an immediate awareness of our advantages in such a way that they would never forget it."

Getting Started

The end result is a selling campaign! A unique slogan, memorable music, and a dazzling combination of words and pictures—all designed to persuade consumers to buy your product. But does it happen? How is that attention-getting and purchase-inducing radio or television commercial actually created?

A commercial is usually written by one or two members of the agency creative department. But it often takes 10, 20, or even more advertiser and agency people to get the copywriter and art director to the point where they have enough information to create an effective commercial. In fact, the writing of a radio or TV spot is the last step in a long creative process that requires the participation of many specialists and can consume a great amount of time.

At the advertising agency, the creative process starts with the formation of an account group

made up of executives from the account management, creative, media, and research departments. The members of the account group are specialists with years of experience in communicating with the consumer. For the advertiser, the process begins with the establishment of a product group, whose area of expertise is the development and marketing of products. Ordinarily, the advertiser product group is made up of a marketing director, a product manager, a product research/development manager, and a marketing research director. The agency account group and the advertiser product group work closely together. Their common goal is to develop an advertising strategy that will lead to the creation of advertising that will solve the product's marketing problem.

The "assignment"—the request from the client for advertising work by the agency—can come in many forms. If the product is new, the assignment will contain marketing objectives, which may be stated in terms of consumer acceptance, dollar sales, share of market, and/or product trial. If the product has been on the market, the assignment may contain revisions of the original objectives or new objectives stated in terms of marketing problems.

For example, research may show that, although consumers like the product, they believe it is not worth the price. Or consumers may consider the product's taste, performance, or durability to be inferior to that of the competition. Or perhaps the product has been hit by a competitive attack on TV that has made people switch brands only because they have been entertained by the competitor's advertising. Whatever the problem, it must be found, analyzed, and defined, usually by the product group. The assignment of solving the problem is then given by the product manager to the agency account manager. In turn, the account manager calls a meeting of the account group, at which the marketing problem is thoroughly discussed and specific tasks are assigned.

Division of Responsibilities

The account manager has the major responsibility for everything the agency does for the client, from advertising strategy to actual commercials. He or she serves as a liaison between the client and every department within the agency. The account manager provides information from the client to these departments and keeps the client abreast of the agency's progress. Because the account manager must make sure that advertiser and agency understand each other, he or she must listen attentively and communicate clearly. And because the account manager is in charge, he or she must organize the project carefully and efficiently.

The creative director, or the assigned copywriter/art director team, is responsible for turning out the finished product. The first task is to find out everything there is to know about the product, the consumer, and the competition. The more questions, the better. Questions lead to hunches. Hunches lead to hypotheses. And hypotheses eventually lead to strategies, which lead to finished radio and television commercials. The creative director must work closely with agency and client research people. He or she must talk to consumers, retailers, and product distributors. Then, after acquiring enough information, the creative director must live and think the product, the consumer, and the competition 24 hours a day, seven days a week.

The research representative of the account group is responsible for gathering secondary and organizing primary research about the product, the consumer, and the competition. He or she should work closely with the creative people assigned to the group to help satisfy their need for information. That information will consist of data supplied by the research people in the product group and by the agency research department's own studies. If primary research is needed, such as focus groups or consumer interviews, the research director may commission an outside research firm.

The media person in the group is assigned the job of finding out what the competition is doing in the various media. How much are they spending? Where? Why? Who is their target market? Are they spending their media money effectively? Is there anything to be learned about the potential customer from his or her media habits? Do media preferences indicate that one medium would work better than others?

The client product group should continue to provide the agency with as much information as possible and to communicate its hunches about the best way to sell the product. Members of the group should be available to answer questions, discuss new thoughts, and generally act as both a catalyst and a sounding board for strategies and ideas throughout the entire course of the project.

Developing the Strategy

Creating a commercial is much like solving a puzzle. And the puzzle is complicated. Who is the person most likely to buy your product? How is he or she influenced by the advertising for competitive products? What is your basic promise to the consumer? Is it strong enough to win customers away from competition? How do you support the promise so that the prospect will believe it? Solving the puzzle—developing the creative or marketing strategy—can take weeks or months. The account group members sometimes resort to brain-storming or other idea-generating techniques. Often, they call in outside experts. They attend many formal meetings and participate in scores of informal discussions. They use research to help test hunches and hypotheses.

One of the most commonly used research methods at this stage in the process is the product concept test. Here, numerous product concepts, sales propositions, are tested with representative samples of the target market. They are simply worded "promises" to consumers indicating what the product can or will do for them. The creative person in the account group writes the various propositions to be tested. These concepts are not phrased as advertising statements. In fact, the less they sound like advertising jargon, the more useful they are.

The creative director (or the creative team) works on developing the "image" of the product. He or she also helps decide which kind of testing will be needed to determine which type of commercial will produce or reinforce the desired image. He or she should be involved in creating and selecting the best "reason why," or supporting statements that will make the selling idea believable. And he or she should participate in choosing the product's brand name, designing the package, writing the label copy, and determining the price—all the elements that help create the product's personality and help support the selling idea.

When all the answers are in, the account group writes a creative or advertising strategy statement (see Exhibits 1—1 and 1–2). This statement should be a one or two page document that

1. Describes the product in real and perceived terms

2. Defines the target customer

3. Defines the competition and what it is saying to the target customer

4. States the one competitive benefit that the product offers the target customer

5. States the support for that benefit

6. Describes the tone of the advertising that will create the brand image of the product

While the strategy statement should be restricted to one page, every section of the statement must be accompanied by a rationale that explains or proves the point being made. The rationale usually contains a definitive analysis of the product, including both product facts and consumer perceptions. The statement should show why the target consumer was chosen over other alternatives. And it should indicate how the competitive promise to the consumer will be supported and made acceptable and believable. One section of the statement should define the objectives of the advertising (what it is expected to accomplish) and the means by which these objectives will be fulfilled (what media will be used to expose the advertising).

Before any advertising is written, the creative or advertising strategy statement must be approved by agency management. After this approval, the strategy must be approved by the client product group.

Finding the Commercial Idea

Once the strategy statement has been approved, the creative director is responsible for creating a commercial that will catch fire with the consumer—a commercial that will be different, better, and successful. So the creative director sets out to deliver the consumer promise, the selling idea, with an unforgettable slogan, a catchy jingle, or a hilarious series of vignettes that will be talked about over morning coffee and honored at award shows. And, in all this, he or she must adhere strictly to the guidelines in the strategy statement.

How does all this happen? The answer is: very slowly and sometimes very painfully. After agency and advertiser approval, the creative director gives the assignment to teams of copywriters and art directors. As the names suggest, the copywriter is responsible for the words and the art director for the pictures and graphics. In practice, however, with talented teams of writers and artists, it is more accurate to say that both are responsible for the "idea" of the commercial. The idea may come from a drawing or a set of words, or both, and it may have been created by either one of the creative team members.

How long does it take to develop the commercial idea? Some creative teams can come up with 30 or 40 ideas in a day. Other teams may develop only one idea in a week. The members of each team can work separately or together. If they decide to split up, they may periodically get together with each other or even with other teams to discuss their ideas. The purpose of such meetings is to try out these ideas on other people. The result is the development of a number of possible ideas that have gone through a series of alterations, adaptations, and refinements.

This period of gestation is also a narrowing-down process. Eventually, inappropriate or unworkable ideas are eliminated, and all the potentially good ones are committed to paper in rough storyboard form. Usually, if the idea is good, you will be able to communicate it with a storyboard that consists of a couple of simply drawn sketches and a few words of copy.

The commercial ideas are then presented by the copywriter and art director teams to the creative director. Ideas that have merit are critiqued, and often changed or fleshed out. Often, more meetings are held to discuss modifications of the original ideas or to consider ideas that may have arisen in the meantime.

Choosing the Right Idea

Creative brainstorming may have produced 20 or 30 rough ideas worth considering. The final refinement stage may have reduced this list to five or six viable ideas. Now it is up to the creative director to make a selection. The decision is not easy. The creative director has to decide which commercials will be recommended to agency and client management and, if approved, eventually produced.

The creative director is usually advised by other members of the account group. Often, the research person tests the selected commercial ideas, even though they are only in preliminary stages of production. This research tries to ascertain whether the points in the creative strategy statement have been made: if the commercial attracts attention, if it appeals to the right consumer, and if it says the right thing—and says it persuasively.

Once the agency approves a commercial, it must be presented to the client. The recommended commercial is usually presented by the copywriter and art director who created it because they know the idea better than anyone else. The finished storyboard or radio script is usually presented with a rationale that tells what the commercial is intended to accomplish, how it will accomplish it, and why, based on research results, it can be expected to accomplish it.

Variations in the Creative Process

The creative process in a large advertising agency generally works in the way described above. But even a small agency or a one-person agency should follow a step-by-step method because it can lead to more effective advertising. However, some agencies may shortcut the process under special circumstances. For example, it is sometimes impractical to take the time and trouble to write a complete strategy statement for a product that the agency is soliciting in a new business presentation; all the marketing data may not be available. And it is not always necessary to devote much time to a successful brand with a minor marketing problem. In such cases, agency and advertiser may choose to update the existing strategy. On the other hand, in marketing a new product, an agency and client may take even more time, use even more people's expertise, and apply the creative process to such areas as product ingredients, quality, design, and performance.

Exhibit 1-1. Strategy Statement: Kwik 'n Kool

PRODUCT: Kwik 'n Kool, distributed by Dunsmore Beverage Co., is a powdered fruit drink. Its granules dissolve in hot or cold water. It contains an artificial sweetener and imitation fruit flavor. There are five Kwik 'n Kool flavors: orange, strawberry, lime, lemon, and Oahu (a combination citrus and pineapple). They taste like natural fruit juices. But Kwik 'n Kool has no health benefit.

Each flavor comes packed in a three- by five-inch flat aluminum foil envelope sealed all around. The name "Kwik 'n Kool" is printed across the face of the front of the package. A picture of the fruit flavor and its name appear on the lower part of the front. Mixing directions are printed on the back. Each package costs 49 cents, 2 cents less than its nearest competitor.

One package makes two quarts. All five flavors can be used together as punch or as the main ingredient of a party punch. Children can easily mix and make Kwik 'n Kool.

Presently, consumers perceive the product as a cheap but nondescript alternative to its costlier and more well-positioned competitors.

CONSUMER: Children 5 to 15 years old account for 90 percent of consumption. Adult use amounts to 3 percent and children in the 16–21 age bracket consume 7 percent. The target market is 8–12 year olds in order to hit the center of the existing market and to establish a uniformly directed advertising campaign.

COMPETITION: Kwik 'n Kool has only 15 percent of the powdered fruit drink market.

The competition includes two powdered drinks (Kool-Aid and Hawaiian Punch), three ready-made drinks (Hawaiian Punch, Capri Sun, and Hi-C), fruit juices, and soft drinks. The direct competitors, the two powdered drink makers, target the low and high end of the 5–15-year-old market, respectively.

COMPETITIVE BENEFIT: Kwik 'n Kool is an easy-to-make, good-tasting, and refreshing summertime drink. However, since the product shares these benefits with competitors, its main competitive difference will be established by its association with children in the designated age group. In addition, although other powdered fruit drinks are equally "quick" and "cool," they have not emphasized these benefits. So advertising should focus on children in the targeted group enjoying both aspects of the product's name.

SUPPORT: These competitive benefits can be stressed by showing children preparing and drinking Kwik 'n Kool while they are having fun. They could be shown taking the package from a kitchen shelf, mixing powder and water, and drinking the results. These events might take place after hard play and before the smiles that indicate satisfaction.

TONE: The advertising should be fast-paced and entertaining. It should establish a clear connection between Kwik 'n Kool and summertime recreation: sports, picnics, vacations. The product should be perceived as the "fun" drink for busy and active children and as indispensable to their free-time activities.

Exhibit 1-2. Strategy Statement: Gro-Slo

PRODUCT: Gro-Slo, a grass-growth inhibitor, is a chemical compound in pellet form. Each pellet is one and one-quarter inches in diameter and has four small holes (arranged like those in a button). Grass-green in color. Toxic. (Pellets should be kept away from children and pets but will not harm them once it has been applied to grass.) A special applicator need be purchased just once. It can be attached to a standard garden hose for application.

Once the Gro-Slo solution is broadcast, the chemical goes to work on leaf and root. It retards the growth of grass—even crab grass. Because the pellets dissolve in water, rain only helps Gro-Slo reach the roots. One application covers 1,000 square feet of lawn. Three applications from April through September should suffice.

CONSUMER: Gro-Slo will be available nationally, but promotional activity will be concentrated in the Southeast. The product will be sold in independent and chain hardware stores, garden centers, and large discount stores. The traditional market for grass-growth inhibitors has been proprietors of golf courses and athletic fields in warm, humid climates, especially in the Southeast. Gro-Slo is aiming for the general consumer market in this region. Potential buyers are middle-income, homeowning males, 35–60 years old, who are concerned about lawn care but are interested in time-saving methods.

COMPETITION: The lone competitor presently promotes the product almost exclusively to golf course owners and grounds maintenance supervisors at schools and colleges. The product, sold in granular form and packaged in 40-pound bags, is less expensive per square foot of application than Gro-Slo, but it is unavailable in retail outlets. It is broadcast by means of a two-wheeled, manual or a full-sized mechanical spreader.

COMPETITIVE BENEFIT: In areas of the country where growing grass is a problem rather than a solution, Gro-Slo can save homeowners time and money. Three applications annually can reduce grass-cutting time by half.

SUPPORT: The benefit can be made credible and attractive by dramatizing the ease and infrequency of application and the reduction in lawn maintenance time resulting from use.

TONE: Although the message can be presented either humorously or seriously, the commercial as a whole should support an image of integrity for the company and of reliability for the product, including both ingredients and applicator. Therefore, if humor is used, it should not be farcical or silly. It must suggest to the audience that, although both company and product are new, they are dependable.

2

Developing the Idea

Writing radio and TV commercials today is in some ways more difficult and in others easier than it was a generation ago. Then, technology was rudimentary. Most commercials, both network and local, were performed live, and experienced writers, actors, and technicians were not always available. Special effects, including music, were often imitative and unsophisticated. Every non-live element had to be performed, cued, and mixed at the very moment the disc or film was being produced. The processing sometimes took days for radio and months for film.

Today, the state of the art has improved dramatically. Participants in both the creation and production of broadcast commercials are specialists in the field. Audio and video tape recording equipment and procedures are virtually flawless. Multitracks are common. Microphones and mixing and editing equipment have been perfected. In TV, lightweight cameras, instant special effects, and computerized optics are almost universally available. Digital technology allows for unlimited changes to originals. Thus, there is more latitude in creativity and production. Creators can do much more, and can do it much better. But this wider choice of talents and techniques also renders decision making far more complicated and therefore far more difficult.

Breaking Through the Clutter

Today, effective radio and television spots must overcome two significant obstacles. First, advertising competition has burgeoned as stations and channels have multiplied. It is much tougher to gain and hold the audience's attention. Second, listeners and viewers have changed. Because of the growing number of advertising impressions in all media, many people have learned, consciously or unconsciously, to block out unwanted sights and sounds. Remote controls allow television viewers to "channel surf" during commercials or to mute the sound during commercial breaks. Loud, repetitive, and simplistic radio and TV spots will simply be ignored or avoided.

In addition, unique problems exist in each medium. People no longer sit in their living rooms quietly and more or less passively listening to the radio as they did in pre-television days. They have radios in just about every room in the house, and they are often doing something other than just listening. A homemaker may be preparing dinner, trying to get the kids off to school, or perhaps just chatting with a neighbor. A teenager may be doing homework, making a snack, or talking on the telephone. In both cases, the listener is unlikely to be riveted to the radio. Furthermore, a commercial may come on as a driver weaves through traffic, a vacationist suns on the beach, a patient waits in a dentist's office, a farmer feeds cattle, a man shaves, or a couple drives on a date. Unlike a TV audience, a radio audience might be anywhere, and its attention is very likely to be divided.

Finally, the person doing the housework might be a man or woman. The many drivers threading through rush-hour traffic may have vastly different tastes and lifestyles. The result is that advertisers compete not only with other advertisers and their products, but also with other activities—some of them totally distracting. And the target audience may not be where you think it is. It may not even be who you think it is.

Radio advertising nevertheless has great selling powers. For this reason, most copywriters happily accept the challenge of both breaking through the competitive clutter and finding the right listener. In fact, the discipline of writing radio commercials under difficult conditions is generally regarded as exceptionally good training. According to Warren Pfaff, former senior vice president of J. Walter Thompson: "If you want to be a good writer, think about radio first. Radio's the little box without eyes, and it doesn't give you an art director to lean on; it doesn't give you any socko picture to bail you out. You're all alone with the listener, and somehow you've got to hit him between the eyes even when his eyes are closed. Once you've learned to do that, you've just got to be a better writer. In any medium."

The need for "breakthrough" writing is just as great in television as it is in radio—perhaps even greater. The double hit of sound and picture can made TV commercials more intrusive and potentially much more annoying than radio. The sheer number of commercials viewers are exposed to is mind-boggling. According to researcher A.C. Nielsen, the average household spends about seven hours a day either watching TV or listening to it, or both. This means that the viewer may see as many as 200 commercials a day. And they come in clusters of six or eight or ten at a time, and in 10, 15, and 30 second general image spots, 1-and 2-minute direct response commercials, and half-hour infomercials—all fighting for a share of the public's mind. The viewer would need a computer to identify, recognize, or remember them.

The television viewing audience has become cynical after years and years of television commercial bombardment. They have set up barriers of disbelief that all TV writers must consider. Viewers have come to distrust even the truth. In addition, because of the look-alike nature of most commercials, brand name recognition among major advertisers is lower than it ever was, despite the millions of dollars spent on getting consumers just to recognize a product's name.

Use Your Research

Agency and client researchers gather facts on every aspect of a product, its market, and its competition. Before you even think of putting pencil to paper, examine this data in relation to the following areas of concern:

1. *Know your customers and prospects.* Who buys your kind of product? Who uses your services? Where? How often? Why? Put yourself in your customers' shoes. Get to know what need might trigger a desire for your product. Is the need emotional? Is the desire practical? Again, ask many questions in your consumer research.

2. *Know your product or service.* Inside and out. What is it? How is it made? What needs does it satisfy? How? What makes it better than the competition? Does it contain any special ingredients? Is it manufactured in an unusual way? Competent research should elicit dozens of such questions. Be sure to get specific answers to all of them.

3. *Know your competition.* What other products or services similar to yours are available? How are they made? What features are better or worse than those of your product? How? Why? Are they virtually the same, as are many cigarettes, beer, and gasoline? Your market and advertising research should explore their selling themes and performance claims. Does competition have a genuine, demonstrable advantage, or has it merely preempted a shared performance characteristic?

When you are satisfied that you know who your customers are, what needs your product satisfies, and how your product compares with competition, you may feel somewhat overwhelmed. But you must have these facts in order to create a sound marketing plan and a clear-cut creative strategy.

Think, Then Write

A creative idea can occur to you at any time after you have absorbed the basic creative strategy. But don't count on "inspiration." An enormous amount of concentrated thought can go into the development of a selling idea. Facts fed into your consciousness boil and turn. They are affected by your subconscious. For example, an idea for an appealing bread commercial awoke David Ogilvy out of a sound sleep. However, much conscious thought had already gone into solving the problem. It is a popular belief that there are no new ideas, only refreshing combinations of old ones, so do not overlook possible combinations or extensions of previously used ideas.

It is a good idea to try out your copy approaches on a friend or coworker. A fresh mind can often spot a strength or weakness that you have failed to see. Better yet, by verbalizing your approach, you may find that you can see an idea in a new light or at a unique angle.

Even experienced pros sometimes run into dry spells. There are ways to get your thoughts going again if you seem to be stuck temporarily. These vary with individuals. Some sleep on the problem. Some take up another chore and return to the problem with fresh perspective. Others flail away at computer and drawing pad and put down dozens of thoughts, almost any thoughts, wild or tame, hopeful that one may lead to the selling idea.

Here is one helpful suggestion. Choose a friend and write him or her a letter (one you probably won't send). Make it sincere, persuasive, and, because this person is your good friend, personal. Try to convince him or her of your product's advantages. Loosen your writing style, be your real self, communicate on a one-to-one basis. Such a relationship, not so incidentally, is the basis of radio and TV selling: Although your audience may number in the millions, you direct your appeal to one person at a time. As your letter develops, you may discover yourself writing about the product in a different, new way.

A gem of an idea may strike you and, figuratively, leap off the page.

Test and Revise

When you feel confident that you have a solid, worthwhile selling idea, compare it with the selling themes of your competitors. Be as objective as you can. Try it out on someone whose opinion you value. Check it against your marketing and advertising objectives. (See Exhibits 2-1 and 2-2.) If it doesn't quite fit, work with variations of the idea. Move words around. Substitute. But always cast it in terms of your prospect's self-interest.

The connotations and denotations of words can be your allies. Just as outstanding chefs can give a special taste to a run-of-the-mill recipe, an imaginative creator of TV or radio spots can bring uniqueness to a selling theme. Words can shock, soothe, stimulate, agitate (even as these words evoke a response in you). Active words, words with vitality, can give your selling theme life and vigor. Be sure that they communicate precisely and truthfully. Make them move your prospect to attention, agreement, acceptance, and action.

If your product's name can become part of the selling idea, you are closer to success. McDonald's uses the first syllable in its name for various products, such as Egg McMuffin and Chicken McNuggets. Meow Mix is advertised as "the cat food cats ask for by name." And as of this writing, the Energizer bunny was still "going...going...going..."

Say It Simply

With a strong selling idea within a memorable theme or phrase, you are ready to give it persuasive shape as a radio or television commercial. The next question to answer is what format the commercial will follow. However, while you may have had some thoughts about format, structure, and style during the development process, it is dangerous to consider such elements before you determine the selling idea. Considering format before content impedes progress toward an effective commercial.

Above all, keep your selling idea easy to understand. Your tag line may be as short as Nike's

"Just Do It." Or it may be as extended as the early FedEx line: "When it absolutely, positively has to be there overnight."

Nike had the dominant share of the exercise shoe market and felt it could defend and grow its franchise by image advertising. Instead of focusing on tangible advantages of its shoes, its advertising said, in effect, "If you don't want to sit on the sidelines, but you want to get active, the right equipment will help you get there. So no excuses! Put on your shoes, go out and just do it."

In the FedEx case, the small-package delivery company was positioned as the one that could be relied on for guaranteed next-day delivery. In essence, the advertising said, "When an important document or small package must arrive, don't take a chance on any other carrier. Use FedEx and you will have the best service and the best guarantee in the business. So your job will never be in jeopardy because a valuable package did not arrive on time."

If a product dominates the category so much that market share cannot be increased, you may be better off selling the category. This is what Campbell's did with, "Soup is Good Food." Polaroid has a similar advantage. But most brands do not hold such a dominant position. So never forget that competition is tough and apt to get tougher. You must get listeners and viewers to recall the product name, remember what the product does, and know how it performs. If you can, include your product's name in the selling theme. "Don't risk it, Wisk it." "My doctor said Mylanta."

Select a Format

Your sales message should come through clearly as your commercial unfolds. The appropriate format should be there to support it, move it along, and give it a framework. If the format draws attention to itself and obscures the product name, it should be changed.

An effective sales theme in a compatible format will help your commercial to attract attention, involve the prospective customer emotionally and logically, develop a desire to try the product, and lead him or her to buy it.

In creating and crafting, make use of your easy access to radio and television spots created by others. By attentive listening and watching, you can become more aware of different selling ideas and how they are presented. As you watch and listen, you should ask a number of questions—and answer them. Are the spots direct and clear? Are they obscure? Do they state benefits? Imply? Do they appeal to emotion or logic?

Questions such as these should be asked when you study the examples of radio and television commercials in Chapters 6 and 9. Note the variety of formats and how the selling ideas are used within them. Be alert to their simplicity, clarity, and strong name identification.

Choose an Appeal

Your TV or radio spot must have a logical or emotional appeal to be successful. If the format can be considered the vehicle, then the appeal can be thought of as the fuel—the energy that makes your vehicle go where you want it to go and do what you want it to do.

Logic might persuade a prospect to buy your product if it outperforms the competition. If your product has parity of performance with the competition, you must search for the one advantage or difference that can be translated into a dramatic sensory or emotional appeal. Health, safety, home, sex, love, and sentiment are strong personal concerns, and ads for products with benefits in these areas should exploit their psychological advantage.

Concern for status evolves from the need for esteem, one of the strongest bases for an emotional appeal. Almost everyone wants to be appreciated, whether by looking better or feeling better. Your research on customer, product, and competition will aid you in discovering other possible appeals.

Humor—Maybe, Maybe Not

Humor is a very popular device, especially with writers of radio spots. But not all uses of humor are effective. Perhaps humor is a favorite with beginning copywriters because it seems easy to write. But real humor is exceedingly difficult to apply to sales messages. Too many radio writers think of themselves as budding Paul Reisers or Jerry Seinfelds, but unless the funny flair sounds spontaneous and original you run the risk of eliciting groans instead of smiles, and no sales will result.

Even spots that are funny on first or second hearing may wear out their welcome quickly. Who listens to and responds to the same joke after half a dozen hearings? It is wiser to make your situation or character funny or amusing by writing it in a warm and engaging style and adding just a touch of irony. But make certain that the selling manner does not overshadow the selling message.

When you produce a humorous spot, cast the voices and direct the tempo with careful regard for timing and inflection. Humor should never sound forced. To succeed, it must be fresh and light.

Imagination—Radio's Big Plus

Writers' and the listeners' imaginations work more effectively in radio advertising than in any other medium. As a radio writer, you are not constrained by the space limitations of print or the linearity of TV. You create mental pictures and activate the imagination of your listeners using sound effects, voices, and music. With audience attention riveted, interest increases, product points gain emphasis, and your spot is on its way to fulfilling its persuasive function.

In radio, you use your kit of audio tools not only to design and set the scene, but also to establish time and place—or immediately change them. In seconds, you can get the listener to picture a cave dweller in prehistory or a Martian in the twenty-second century. In one of Stan Freberg's best radio spots, an "on-the-scene" announcer excitedly described a thousand airplanes flying over Lake Michigan and dropping tons of cherries onto a frothy mountain of whipped cream. The "set" cost nothing. It was simply the product of a rich and bountiful imagination.

Another of radio's most inventive (and award-winning) copywriters, Chuck Blore, claims that there is nothing that cannot be done on radio, at least "visually." According to copywriter Larry Rood, "Radio is the most visual of all media. You can create characters, situations, whole worlds that can't be duplicated on TV or in print. When you create this imaginary situation, the listener can project himself into that world through imagination."

To draw the listener in, your commercial must trigger his or her imagination, participation, and involvement. Unless your commercial succeeds, in this, it will not succeed in meeting its marketing and advertising goals.

TV—The Power of Technology

Commercials on TV have been around for half a century, yet every day we see new techniques, such as surrealistic computer animation and creative use of black-and-white photography, designed to overwhelm the viewer with a dramatic impression of the product. Technologically, there is little in the way of special effects that cannot be achieved on film or videotape. The exciting fantasies used in films like *Terminator 2, True Lies, Jurassic Park,* and *Forrest Gump* are available for use in commercials. Every scene your imagination can envision can be put on film for the world to see. Even scenes your mind cannot dream up can be electronically created by computers, which can be programmed to generate new forms of graphics and animation. The advent of videotape and "fast film" makes it possible to shoot practically anything, anywhere, at any time, day or night.

The new techniques are exciting, but they are also very expensive. Some of them force the cost of commercials into millions of dollars. The true challenge to the creative person working in TV is to come up with fresh, innovative ideas that do not depend entirely on advanced technology. The second challenge is to search continually for new film, tape, animation, or computer techniques that are both provocative and relatively inexpensive.

What Is a "Good" Commercial?

In just one day, a TV viewer may be exposed to hundreds of commercials. Over a year, tens of thousands. In 1992, advertisers spent 29 billion dollars buying air time to run TV commercials.

Numbers like these mean that one of the principal requirements of a "good" commercial is that it must stand out from the crowd. If it does not, the advertiser is losing money.

Research shows that most people do not mind television or radio advertising in general, although they dislike certain commercials. They do not like to be yelled at or treated rudely. They want to be respected. And that is what a good commercial should do. It should be a friend rather than an intruder. It should be welcome every time it comes into someone's home.

A good commercial is honest. It should express the creative strategy in a highly believable manner. If your commercial is insincere or untrue, your customer may spot it in an instant. And even if it takes longer for him or her to find out that you have been deceptive or misleading or downright dishonest, the result will be the same: declining sales and perhaps irreparable damage to your client's (and your own) reputation.

A good commercial is positive. It should leave your potential customer with a favorable impression of the product. And it should make the viewer or listener feel good about the company that makes the product. Avoid negative implications, and take advantage of every opportunity to show the product and the company in the best possible light.

A good commercial is persuasive. It should get people to buy the product and make them more likely to enjoy it when they use it. Remember, it is not enough to win prizes. You are not selling yourself, your creative talent, or even your commercial. You are selling your client's product or service. And if you do not persuade the consumer to buy it, you are wasting your time and your client's money.

A good commercial is simple. When audiences hear or see a commercial, they have one question in mind: "What's in it for me?" The less effort they have to expend in getting the answer to this question, the more effort they are likely to use in buying the product. Most commercials are too complicated structurally and too involved verbally. The best advertising creative people have one thing in common: a working knowledge of the fine art of omission. They do only what is necessary, and they do that succinctly and competently.

A good commercial is specific. It should make one definite point and support it with concrete evidence. Use numbers if you can. And explain product design or ingredients if they are distinctive or important. Avoid relying on general impressions and vague themes.

A good commercial talks person to person. It should not be addressed to broad demographic groups, such as working women or school children or retirees. It should not even appeal to specific product users, such as car owners or bran cereal buyers. It should talk to one man or woman or child who has a problem, and it should show how your product can solve that person's problem.

A good commercial makes a promise. Whether it is logical or emotional, however, the promise must be related to the product. It does not have to be in the form of a sentence or a statement. In some cases, a picture will do as well—or better. Or the promise can be suggested or implied by the story you tell or by the tone you convey.

A good commercial builds a personality for the product. Of course, this is a long-term process. But once you have decided on a particular identity or image, stick to it by making sure that every TV or radio spot contributes to it consistently and directly.

A good commercial does the unexpected. If some of the other virtues of good advertising seem obvious to you, remember to combine them with surprise. Too many advertisers cling to outmoded, derivative, or stereotyped forms, as do many timid or unimaginative copywriters and art directors. But the goal is not to satisfy the creative person's desire to show his or her creative prowess.

The commercial should perform the extremely useful task of making certain that the advertiser's product will not be lost in the huge swamp of ho-hum advertising.

Advertisers continually strive to produce good commercials. And there is a point at which advertising stops being a craft and comes as close as it can to being an art. What makes the difference is hard to determine. The operative word, probably, is "vitality." The superior commercial starts out as an inspired idea. Then it strikes a chord with its viewers or listeners and takes on a life of its own as it hits the airwaves or the TV screen. And later, long after the commercial has run and the campaign is over, it is still remembered with a certain mixture of awe and appreciation.

Exhibit 2-1. Marketing Objectives: Sears

Marketing: Sears has a long-established reputation as a source for appliances, auto parts, tools, and other hard goods. Build store traffic by creating awareness among female shoppers of Sears being a resource for contemporary and stylish clothing and accessories.

Advertising: Use the consumers' knowledge of Sears "hard" products in a creative way to communicate that Sears also sells a wide variety of desirable "soft" goods.

Advertiser: Sears

Agency: Young & Rubicam New York

Product: Apparel Brand

Title: "Hey Mister"

Format: Musical/Vignettes

Length: 60 seconds

SINGER: Hey Mister,

Your hardware's looking real good.

These power belts are cool.

Copper cables

and silverware.

Ooh, I'm strappin' on these tools.

'Cause you'll be the first place

I'll always try,

'cause hardware now has a softer side.

As I look now, you look new.

For electric pumps, I'll come to you.

What's good you're making better.

Seems like

we still belong together.

Yeah, yeah, you'll be the first place I'll always try,

'cause hardware now

has a softer side.

(MUSIC)

Come see the softer side of Sears.

(MUSIC OUT)

Exhibit 2–2. Marketing Objectives: Xerox

Marketing: To expand the use of Xerox machines to central reproduction centers characterized by high-volume duplicating. To compete in this market, a new high-speed machine with automatic collating capability was developed.

Advertising: To establish awareness of the new copier. To communicate that Xerox is an advanced technology company, a good corporate citizen, and a company whose advertising is distinctive and memorable.

Advertiser: Xerox Corp.

Agency: Needham, Harper & Steers, Inc.

Product: Xerox 9200 Duplicating System

Title: "Monks"

Format: Problem/Solution

Length: 60 seconds

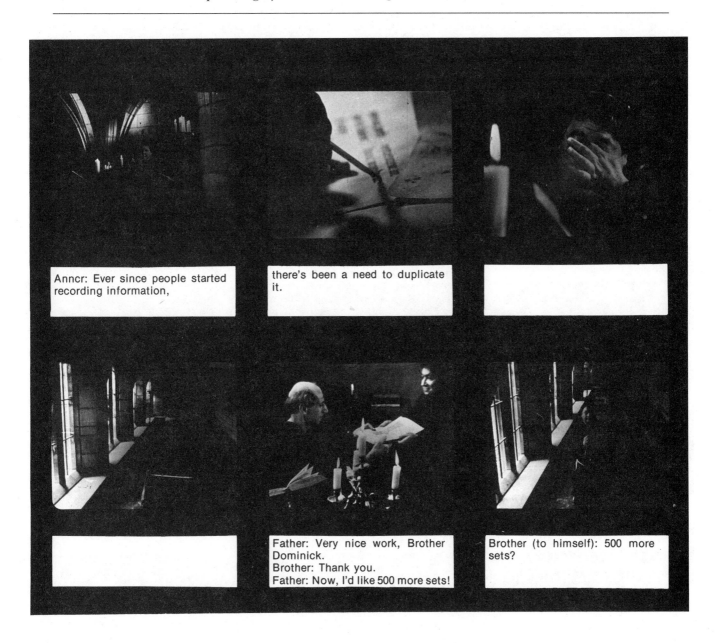

Anncr: Ever since people started recording information,

there's been a need to duplicate it.

Father: Very nice work, Brother Dominick.
Brother: Thank you.
Father: Now, I'd like 500 more sets!

Brother (to himself): 500 more sets?

Stephens: Brother Dominick, what can I do for you?

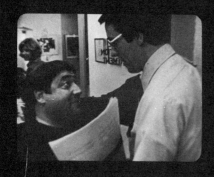

Brother: Could you do a big job for me?

Announcer, V.O.: Xerox has developed an amazing machine that's unlike anything we've ever made. The Xerox 9200 Duplicating

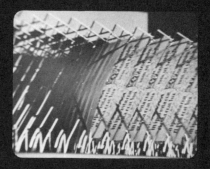

System. It automatically feeds and cycles originals . . . Has a computerized programmer that coordinates the entire system.

Can duplicate, reduce and assemble a virtually limitless number of complete sets . . .

Brother: Here are your sets, Father.
Father: What?
Bro.: The 500 sets you asked for.

Father: It's a miracle!

3

Choosing the Format

Viewers and listeners certainly are capable of being attracted by, paying attention to, and absorbing sales messages. However, there is no reason to assume that at any given time *your* audience is either ready or willing to watch or hear *your* commercial.

Your prospective customers may be distracted by worries, needs, or concerns that have nothing to do with your product. They may be so intensely engaged in thinking, planning, daydreaming, problem solving, or reminiscing that no selling idea can break through to consciousness. Or prospects may be reluctant to accept your request for 30 seconds of attraction, attention, and absorption because they are hungry or bored or impatiently waiting for a favorite program to resume.

Yet, despite these obstacles, your commercial must somehow do its job. And it must not only capture your prospects' interest, but also fix your selling message in their minds, gain confidence, and motivate a purchase decision.

Obviously, these objectives can be attained only if your communication is stimulating and relevant and presented in an orderly way. Ideas that are arranged coherently, developed logically, and conveyed clearly are easier to understand, accept, and remember than are ideas that are unrelated to each other, randomly ordered, and smothered by an attention-getting style or an obtrusive technique.

The Main Idea

You must be careful never to overload a commercial with too many selling facts or too large a variety of styles or techniques. If a commercial tries to use too many ideas, words and pictures will emerge haphazardly and ineffectively. Such a commercial is likely to join the 85 percent of all advertisements that, according to William Bernbach, go completely unnoticed.

The importance of presenting simple messages in a clear-cut form has been demonstrated in the studies of Gallup & Robinson, a prominent research organization. These investigations into commercial effectiveness indicate that viewer and listener recall is lessened when multiple ideas are crammed into a TV or radio message. Keep your commercial focused and give it a sound structure.

Perhaps it is obvious that a 10-second station-break announcement (or I.D.) should contain only one selling idea. With only 8 seconds of audio at your disposal, you have only enough time for a basic claim or selling idea and the product or company name. As you create 20-second, or 30-second, one-minute, and two-minute spots, you will be able to include more entertainment and information. But even in the longer commercials the selling idea is still the prime mover of your prospective customer. A good test of a selling idea, in fact, is to make it work effectively in a short spot. Some ingenious advertisers use in their I.D.s shortened forms of the same elements that they use for their longer commercials.

The commercial examples in Chapter 6 and 9 demonstrate how and where some of today's top creators of commercials implant the main idea, support it, and, in some cases, restate it. From opening fade-in to closing fade-out, the basic selling proposition in the best commercials moves progressively within a carefully chosen format and tautly conceived structure.

Formats

In this book, the term "format" refers to the major types of commercials. The word "structure" is used to indicate the temporal sequence or arrangement within a commercial. Some formats—such as problem-solution, narrative, slice of life, and demonstration—have their own definite structure. You begin with a problem and end with a solution. You tell a story with a beginning, a middle, and an end. You dramatize the discovery of a product feature or consumer benefit. Or you show the step-by-step process of using the product. Other formats can be structured in a variety of ways. And all formats can be done in any style and aided by any technique.

Your choice of format will depend on a number of considerations: the product or service, the market, the audience, the production budget, the intended number of exposures of the commercial, the competition, and so on. Some structures are better suited to certain kinds of products and are entirely wrong for others. Obviously, a problem-solution structure works best for products that can actually solve problems—laundry detergents, but not designer clothes. A narrative structure, in which a special mood is created, is appropriate for products that appeal to the senses—perfumes, but not hardware. A demonstration can be effective for products with benefits that must be shown rather than described—small kitchen appliances, but usually not such consumer packaged goods as orange juice, soap, and cat food.

The danger in classifying commercials by format is that it seems to codify creativity and limit experimentation. So this disclaimer is needed:

The formats described here do not by any means constitute a definitive or exhaustive list.

Furthermore, as you begin to analyze commercials, you will note that some of them use more than one format. (See the exhibits at the end of this chapter.) For example, a basic problem-solution commercial can be set in a fantasy scene and include a brief demonstration of the product. Most of the formats are not mutually exclusive. However, one format usually dominates. Another can be treated as an additional—and subordinate—element.

Problem-Solution Format
The problem-solution format is a story-telling genre. Structurally, the problem must come first, the solution second. And both must be presented dramatically. The problem must seem important and evoke a negative response from the central actor or actors—worry, fear, discomfort, or dissatisfaction. When the product is introduced, whether it is merely shown or briefly demonstrated, it should solve the problem and result in relief, pleasure, or satisfaction.

The problem-solution format differs from the slice-of-life format in that it focuses on 1) a specific problem—plaque (Oral B), hemorrhoids (Preparation H), or sinusitis (Sine-Aid); 2) a specific product feature that represents the solution—unique shape toothbrush, medicine to shrink sensitive swollen tissues, maximum strength medicine that doesn't cause drowsiness; and 3) a specific consumer benefit—no more embarrassment, no more discomfort, no more pain or drowsiness.

Appropriate products for the problem-solution format are those that actually do something—and presumably do it better than other products: laundry detergents, household cleaners, toothbrushes, deodorants, and headache remedies. However, products whose primary feature is usually perceived by the senses—that is, products that would otherwise be treated in a slice-of-life format—can be positioned as problem-solvers: for example, bathroom tissue in a longer roll (Scott), soap with high cold cream content (Dove), or low-cholesterol margarine (Fleischmann's). In such cases, the selected feature is usually quantifiable: 50 more sheets, 25 percent moisturizing cream, made with pure vegetable oil.

The problem-solution format differs from the narrative commercial in that the actors might talk directly to the audience, a voice-over announcer might introduce the product, and special-effects devices might be used to enhance the entrance or demonstration of the product. There is little attempt to maintain a particular mood or atmosphere. So, when the point is made—that is, when the problem is either clarified or solved—the problem-solution commercial often breaks from the dramatized situation in order to underscore the selling message. The sell may be "hard," but it can be softened by a humorous treatment. Because the problem-solution structure is so widely used, it must be carefully crafted to avoid the appearance of triteness or sameness.

Slice-of-Life Format

The most popular format in commercials is the slice-of-life, because it is so effective. In the slice-of-life format you develop a "plot" with a beginning, middle, and end. A typical slice has two people in a real-life setting, such as a kitchen. One has a problem and is the "doubter." The other, who knows the product can solve the problem, is the "convincer." Casting is critical in a slice of life commercial. Good actors will be required to make the dialogue sound believable. It helps if they have memorable faces, voices, and mannerisms, as well. The dialogue and situation should be as believable as possible, not contrivances that would never occur in real life. A dramatic opening should visualize the problem the product solves. For example, an effective opening scene for a Children's Tylenol commercial was a sad-faced toddler who trudged into her parents' bedroom in the middle of the night and exclaimed, "Mommy, I feel hot." Mommy comforted her daughter while she told daddy (the doubter, who thought aspirin was indicated) to get the Children's Tylenol. The next morning the story had a happy ending when the little girl's fever was gone.

This format also fits products whose product feature is general rather than specific and abstract rather than concrete: reliability (Maytag), good service (Kinko's), or high quality (Sony). In fact, the "problem" in a slice-of-life commercial may be a matter of sense-perception, and the "solution" may be highly subjective. The commercial may begin with a character who expresses a desire for a product that tastes better, feels softer, or looks more attractive. However, this desire need not be articulated. The slice-of-life format requires only that this expressed or unexpressed wish to be fulfilled, usually by a discovery either prompted by a friend, relative, or neighbor, or resulting from accidental trial.

In this kind of commercial, the emphasis is usually on a product feature rather than a consumer benefit. The feature, though shared with other products in the category, may be selected in order to give a parity product—facial tissue, food, soap—a special identity or a special "position" in the marketplace.

Therefore, the commercial may focus on a somewhat indeterminate selling point: "mountain-grown" flavor in Folger's coffee, mildness in Palmolive dishwashing liquid, or butterlike taste in Parkay margarine. Furthermore, the product feature may be implied rather than expressed.

The danger in the slice-of-life format is that the message may be lost because of too much vagueness or indirectness. For this reason, the plot should be simple and clear. Each step in the story should relate to the point that has gone before. Interest should be built gradually, and the outcome should come as a surprise. In addition, if the taste, feel, or look of the product depends on uniqueness of ingredients, structure, or design, this point should be emphasized. If the treatment is humorous, the punch line or visual surprise should relate to the product, its features, or its benefits.

Burlesque Format

Burlesque is a humorous exaggeration of reality. It answers the question: "What is the best (or worst) thing that can happen as a result of using (or not using) this product?" For instance, Maytag appliances last so long that the repairman is very lonely. FedEx built its reputation by exaggerating what could happen if a package was not delivered on time. In a Stroh's beer commercial, a "good-taste" message was dramatized by the sound of an off-stage dog lapping up the contents of a beer bottle that the dog had removed from the refrigerator when asked to do so by its on-stage, card-playing owner. The discovery was that the beer is so good that even dogs can't resist it.

Keep in mind that while your audience will reject unreality, they will accept an extreme exaggeration of reality, as long as it is based on their beliefs. So when Michael Jordan and Larry Bird compete for a Big Mac by getting "nothing but net" as they shoot baskets from "across the Milky Way," we gladly go along with the fun. We also take away the message that top athletes think a meal at McDonald's is very good, indeed.

However, burlesque is not appropriate to every product category. Alka Seltzer learned this some years back when wonderfully funny commercials lost market share. One classic spot showed a newlywed husband suffering through his bride's first attempts at cooking, which included such things as "poached oysters." The commercial was very funny. But people in pain do not want to laugh, nor do they want their ailments trivialized. They want relief.

If you attempt to burlesque, do not make fun of your product. You are on much safer ground if you poke fun at what can happen if people do not use it, or if they use the competition's product. Also, do not make fun of your customers. Instead, you might illustrate the steps people will take to acquire the product, such as the "Yes I am" impersonator who goes to such lengths for a Bud Light.

Narrative Format

A narrative commercial tells a story. Unlike the slice-of-life commercial, however, it attempts to create a situation that is highly personal, emotionally strong, and deeply involving. In the endeavor to create a mood, the narrative (or story-line) commercial may completely ignore all product features and focus exclusively on a consumer benefit. In fact, even the benefit may be only indirectly related to the product.

The classic Lowenbrau "Here's to Good Friends" commercials identified their beer with leisure, relaxation, and fellowship. AT&T's "Reach Out and Touch Someone" campaign associated long-distance calling with friendship and family ties. Campbell's "Soup for Lunch" spots said nothing about the taste, price, nutrition, or quality. They stressed the warmth of mother-son relationships aided by a midday serving of hot soup.

The narrative commercial may deal with a problem, as in Hallmark card spots where a dreary day was made brighter with a greeting card from a friend or relative. However, the problem is often emotional—frustration, loneliness, disappointment—and the soft-sell solution may be communicated in a smile, a handshake, or a pat on the back, rather than a summary of product features or consumer benefits, which usually comes at the end of a problem-solution commercial. In an award-winning spot for Coca-Cola, for example, a young fan asked football star "Mean Joe" Green for his autograph, got turned down, offered Joe a Coke, and got a smile and a T-shirt in return. The features (tasty and thirst-quenching), as well as the benefits (satisfaction and refreshment), were submerged under the less tangible but more touching aura of gratitude and human decency. Pepsi-Cola did a funny send-up of this spot in which a youngster refused to share his soda with a famous athlete.

Because the narrative format rests so heavily on atmosphere, every attempt must be made to sustain the emotion-generating "feel" of the commercial. The spot should begin and end with the story intact. And the concluding product-identifying voice-over or jingle must not break the spell. Unlike the slice-of-life commercial, the narrative commercial calls for little or no dialogue, understated acting, and characters who not only induce audience identification, but also create sympathy and elicit involvement.

Demonstration Format

Television can show a product in a way that no other mass communication medium can. From the very beginning, TV advertising has taken advantage of this opportunity. In the 1950's, a device for slicing and dicing and otherwise preparing vegetables for cooking was frequently demonstrated on late-night television. More recently, similar products—such as the Cuisinart, as well as personal computers and office copiers—have been demonstrated in prime time.

Effective demonstrations hold attention, prove a product's workability or superiority, and convince the viewer to buy. And, of course, they score extremely well in terms of audience involvement. In fact, there is no better way to overcome sales resistance. All research shows this.

Nothing sells a prospective customer faster and more compellingly than actually showing that a product does what it is supposed to do.

Demonstrations are particularly appropriate for products that are genuinely different from others and whose difference is in how they work, rather than in how they look, taste, or feel. The commercial can show the product in action, if this is the product's strongest selling point. Or it can focus on a variety of applications, if this is the thrust of the sales message.

However, the demonstration is not limited to technological wonders that perform extraordinary feats, such as hand-held vacuum cleaners, torture-tested wristwatches, and high-speed office copiers. This format can also be used to demonstrate special features of ordinary products, such as thickness in catsup, lack of greasiness in potato chips, and durability in kitchen utensils.

In a demonstration spot the feature or benefit is actually demonstrated rather than merely explained, either by normal filming or taping or by time-lapse or before/after photography for slow-working products, such as house paints, grass seed, microwave ovens, and cake mixes. A discussion of how something works—describing its ingredients, structure, or design—is not a demonstration.

If you use a demonstration, however, you must be absolutely certain that your performance claim is true and that the demonstration itself is authentic. For example, in a long-running spot for Denorex anti-dandruff shampoo, a man lathered up one side of his head with Denorex and the other side with another shampoo. He comments that the side with the Denorex gives him a tingling sensation. The implication is that Denorex is more effective against dandruff. In reality, the tingling is due to the fact that Denorex contains menthol, which does nothing to fight dandruff.

Product Alone Format

A spot that shows the product by itself can be easy to produce and therefore relatively low-cost. You let the viewer look at the product—presumably because it is beautiful, new, or different—while the voice-over announcer tells what it is, what it has (or doesn't have), and what it does.

However, because few products can sustain 30 or 60 seconds of visual attention, advertisers often turn to camera or computer tricks to hold interest. In the early days of television, a woman dressed in an oversized pack of Old Gold cigarettes with only her legs showing tap-danced her way into the hearts and lungs of America. The connection between product and commercial content was tenuous, but the spot had considerable staying power because it offered an unusual variation on the product-alone format.

This format can be used for products that have some inherent drama, such as new products, old products in a new form or package, or products that are pleasing to the eye. When Contac cold-remedy capsules were introduced, the TV commercials showed, in slow motion and close up, "tiny time pills" spilling out of the capsule. Burger King filled the TV screen with a shot of the Whopper, followed by a series of vignettes showing each ingredient of the sandwich. And aesthetically pleasing products, such as automobiles, often use this format.

Perfumes have flowed gently out of their artfully designed bottles; models have gracefully descended spiral staircases in mink coats; and Michelob beer, accompanied by minimal voice-over copy, has been dramatically poured into a pilsner glass to the strains of a triumphant melody, for which the only lyric was the repeated word "Michelob."

When the product or package innovation requires explanation, the voice-over announcer can describe the product in detail. Alternatively, when visual appeal is emphasized, the commercial may begin or end with a theme statement and allow the strong video to do the talking. Burger King, for example, began with the statement that the following presentation of the Whopper was intended to test the power of hungry viewers to resist the appetizing allure of the hamburger. The close: "We hope we won't have to do this again." Michelob beer concluded its slow-motion video with the tag "Some things speak for themselves."

Table top spots (in which the product is shown on top of a table) can go with minimal copy, as in some cereal commercials, or with extensive description, as in food commercials offering free recipes.

Although radio may seem to be an unlikely medium for "showing" the product alone, it can work for products whose primary use is auditory:

recording equipment, records and tapes, concerts, and stereo components. Radio has also been used to transmit the sounds of beer pouring, car engines humming, and soft drinks fizzing. Whenever the sound of a product is easily recognizable, it can be transmitted on radio. In fact, some products that have become identified with a unique sound—Alka-Seltzer (plop, plop, fizz, fizz), Tums (tum-ta-tum-tum), and Kellogg's Rice Krispies (snap, crackle, and pop)—are particularly good candidates for product-alone radio treatment.

A subcategory of the product-alone format is the analogy, in which either the product or the use of the product is presented analogically or symbolically. An analogy is defined as "a relation of likeness between two things." The likeness is not between the things themselves, however, but between "two or more attributes, circumstances, or effects." In an analogical commercial, you would use something with a quality or attribute that relates to your product. Bulls have been used to symbolize the "power" of malt liquor and the upswinging stock market for an investment firm. Drinking a rosé wine has been compared to "taking a trip to Portugal." The speed and sleekness of a car have been compared to those qualities in a race horse. For the viewer to make the (sometimes implicit) connection, the analogy must be clear and relevant. Audiences are often unwilling to exert the effort that is necessary to follow a complicated comparison, so the analogy should be relatively simple and logically, as well as emotionally, acceptable.

Spokesperson Format

The use of an on-camera announcer to speak directly to television viewers about a sponsor's product dates from the first days of television. In its simplest form, it is a straight radio announcement illustrated by a moving picture of the announcer and the product. Although it is sometimes enlivened by a demonstration, it is basically "talk," which may be fast and hard sell or personal and intimate.

Direct communication between a spokesperson and the audience is a valuable and generally economical device. The message is straightforward and simple; there is little to distract the viewer or listener from learning about the product and finding out why he or she should buy it. The spokesperson may discuss product features or consumer benefits, or present the product in a problem-solution structure.

Whatever the formal structure may be, this type of commercial has the force of the spokesperson's personality behind it. Many effective network commercials use a "name" announcer. These are the qualities that give this format its selling strength.

The spokesperson can be a salesperson representing the sponsor, the president of the company, or an actor or actress playing either. Lee Iacocca, head of Chrysler Corp., was an effective spokesman for his company. Airlines and automakers have used a variety of actual employees to discuss the virtues of their products or services.

The spokesperson can also be an expert—say, a nutrionist, a car mechanic, a dishwasher—or, again, an actor or actress playing these roles. He or she can be a well-known movie star, public figure, or professional athlete. Here, however, product and spokesperson must be carefully matched. Sexy film stars touting auto transmissions or hardware products may not be as effective as celebrities who can be identified with the product. When the president of the Hair Club for Men revealed that he was balding and said, "I'm also a customer," he hit a responsive chord. So did Victor Kiam, who told us he liked Remmington Electric Shavers so much, "I bought the company." Sports Illustrated accomplished the same thing with their exercise videos with swimsuit models Cheryl Tiegs, Elle Macpherson, and Rachel Hunter.

Even if celebrities are not part of the product, a concept should be built around them. It was difficult to imagine anyone but Ray Charles singing, "You Got the Right One Baby, Uh-Huh." In fact, one of the spots in this campaign spoofed other entertainers auditioning for the role. Similarly, Bob Vila, who hosts a TV show for do-it-yourselfers, was a good choice as the spokesman for the Time-Life Books series on home improvements. Here the use of the celebrity was driven by the concept, as it should be.

The personality spokesperson is an actor or actress who plays a role written especially for the product. This variant relies on a performer (often a comedian or comic actor) who can command attention and interest with a distinctive characterization—a unique voice, delivery, or appearance.

Testimonial Format

Word-of-mouth advertising is one of the most effective ways of calling attention to a product. It comes from people who have used a product and liked it. The testimonial is an attempt to capture the persuasiveness of this kind of advertising. Like the spokesperson, the testifier speaks directly to the audience. However, instead of talking about the product, the spokesperson discusses his or her experience with it.

Testimonials can be delivered by either celebrities or unknowns. Famous people can give your commercial special appeal. And if the spot as a whole is informative, entertaining, and promising, the extra cost can be worth it. Again, however, product and testifier must go together. The viewer or listener must believe that the celebrity has actually used the product and is really expressing his or her own feelings about it. When Julia Louis-Dreyfus, Rachel Hunter, or Cindy Crawford talk to us about their shampoo, perfume, lipstick, or cosmetics, we have no reason not to believe them. On the other hand, when Jaclyn Smith tells us she shops at K Mart, and Kathie Lee Gifford accidentally bumps into Regis Philbin aboard a Carnival Cruise Line ship, we may have reason to doubt.

On the other hand, an unknown person who recommends a product is probably less subject to the suspicion that he or she is merely endorsing the product for a fee. Furthermore, audiences often respond favorably to peer recommendations. An average consumer in a store, a home, or a garage can recommend a detergent, a rug cleaner, or an oil filter and create credibility.

Some years back, several bottles of Tylenol pain reliever capsules were found to be laced with strychnine. The product was pulled from drug store and supermarket shelves nation wide. The company presented a series of testimonials featuring responsible-looking wives and mothers who convincingly underlined the PR-motivated campaign theme: trust. As far as the audience could tell, these women were long-time users of the product. And their naturalness and sincerity helped restore Tylenol to its position as category leader.

A testimonial can be structured in narrative, slice-of-life, or problem-solution form. The camera can be hidden to catch spontaneity and convey authenticity. The commercial can also be presented as an interview. When the testifier uses his or her own words, the testimonial is more plausible and persuasive.

Musical Format

In television, the musical spot consists of a vocal or instrumental sound track accompanied by a performance of the music, either just singing or both singing and dancing. In radio, it is only a song. In both media, the music should be catchy and upbeat, attention-getting and entertaining. Music can create a mood, as in George Gershwin's "Rhapsody in Blue" for United Airlines, and lyrics can attempt to change an image, as in "Come See the Softer Side of Sears."

Musical products, such as CDs, music videos, stage shows, rock concerts, and symphonic or operatic productions are especially well suited to musical treatment. The format best fits any product that at a particular time seems to need a splashy, spectacular presentation. Thus, many product introductions, revivals, and repositionings have been set to elaborate song-and-dance numbers. And the same is true of products undergoing a special promotion—sweepstakes, price cuts, and special events (especially holiday celebrations). Music can even work in direct response. "Time Flies" was a very effective song for *TIME* magazine.

Certain mass-appeal, quasi-parity products, such as soft drinks and fast food, have turned to the musical format again and again. RC Cola ran a series of narrative-video/musical-audio spots under the theme "Me and My RC." Coca-Cola had a large, international-looking group of children line up along a horizon and sing, "I'd like to buy the world a Coke." Dr. Pepper used a lead singer/dancer and a group of spectators (who finally got into the act) to urge its youthful target market to "Be a Pepper."

The jingle is a miniature version of the musical, and its brevity requires that it be used as a framing device or as a closing signature. However, music can also be used to enhance a dramatic moment in an emotionally engaging narrative or to create atmosphere for any kind of dramatization. When the characters in a narrative actually act out the lyrics of a song and the song runs the entire length of the spot, the commercial is a musical because the audio determines the content of the video. When the music, whether vocal or instrumental, supports the story, the commercial is what it is by virtue of its video content.

A Final Warning

Although the formats discussed here cover the territory fairly well, the most common commercial on television is not adequately described by any of them. It is a combination of continuous music, voice-over narration, and storytelling video. The latter is usually a series of vignettes that fall into the slice-of-life or problem-solution category. The difficulty with such commercials is not that they are unclassifiable. It is that they are too cluttered, burdened as they are with too many elements, each of which fights for attention and none of which dominates.

Too often, the result is a commercial that is unclear and ineffective. Make it easy for your prospective viewer or listener. Choose a format or a combination of formats. But develop the ad clearly and logically. Do not weigh it down with too many ideas or elements. Remember that the format itself will neither compel nor sell. But as you develop your selling idea within the framework of a format, do not add too much. Keep the sales message in the forefront of your mind and in the foreground of your commercial.

When you watch TV or listen to the radio, notice and evaluate each commercial's format. Note which ones have well-defined formats and which ones do not. The best-remembered and most effective spots will usually be those with strong selling ideas and well-chosen formats.

Exhibit 3–1. Mixed Formats: Goodyear

Advertiser: Goodyear

Agency: J. Walter Thompson

Product: Aquatred tires

Title: "Bucket"

Format: Spokesperson/Demonstration

Length: 30 seconds

AQUATRED

GTBM-9943

(MUSIC THROUGHOUT)
ANNCR: (VO) This is a Goodyear
Aquatred and this is a gallon of water.

At highway speeds in a rain storm,

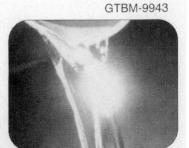

Goodyear Aquatred

pumps a gallon of water every second
thanks to its computer designed "deep
groove" Aquachannel.

It channels water away as you drive

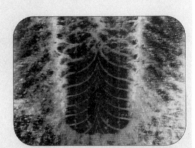

to keep more of the tire in contact with
the road

for outstanding wet-weather traction.

It's only from Goodyear.

And it comes with a 60,000 mile
treadlife warranty.

The all-season   Aquatred.   Try a set.

We like to say: The best tires in the world have
                       Goodyear written all over them.

Exhibit 3-2. Mixed Formats: S.O.S.

Advertiser: Miles Laboratories

Agency: Doyle Dane Bernbach, Inc.

Product: S.O.S. scouring pads

Title: "New York Ladies"

Format: Slice of life/Demonstration/Comparison

Length: 30 seconds

(SFX: CLANG OF POT)
S.O.S LADY: (OFF CAMERA) Grace is that you?

BRILLO LADY: No, it's Miss America. I'm here doing dishes between appearances.

S.O.S LADY: (LAUGHS) Still with the jokes. Listen, did you get S.O.S?
BRILLO LADY: No.

S.O.S LADY: No!? But I told you it's better than Brillo.
BRILLO LADY: I know.

S.O.S LADY: The soap lasts longer.
BRILLO LADY: I know.

S.O.S LADY: And it cuts grease quicker than Brillo.
BRILLO LADY: I know.

S.O.S LADY: So, Grace, S.O.S could get you out of the kitchen faster.

(SFX: CRUNCH!!!)

BRILLO LADY: Who wants to get out of the kitchen faster?

Exhibit 3–3. Mixed Formats: Union 76

Advertiser: Union Oil Co. of California   **Title:** "Thanks, Nick"
Agency: Leo Burnett U.S.A.   **Format:** Spokesman/Slice of Life/Musical
Product: Union 76 Unleaded Regular gasoline   **Length:** 60 seconds

---

SING: YOU'RE ROLLIN' DOWN THE HIGHWAY
THERE'S SO MUCH OUT THERE TO SEE

NICK: Hi, I'm Nick, from Murph's Seventy-Six. And I'm hearing a lot of "Thank-You's" lately.

VOICE 1:   Hey, Nick, thanks! You saved me money!

NICK: See?

VOICE 2:   Yeah, Nick—I really didn't need premium unleaded to quiet those knocks and pings! Thanks, buddy.

NICK: Noo problem. Oh, the reason for the "Thanks-You's" is Union Seventy-Six Unleaded Regular. It's the unleaded with the big plus...more spirit. Seventy-Six Unleaded has more spirit than other unleaded regulars.

VOICE 3:   Thanks, Nick!

NICK: Anytime! Listen, if your car's knocking and pinging and you're thinkin' you might have to pay for premium unleaded...try Union Seventy-Six Unleaded Regular instead. You'll recognize it by the big plus on the pump. It tells you about the big plus that's been inside our gasoline for a long time...more spirit. Try it...you might thank me, too.

SEXY FEMALE: Thanks, Nick...

NICK: Sure...gulp...You're welcome...

SING: COME IN AND GO WITH THE SPIRIT
THE SPIRIT OF SEVENTY-SIX

4

Structure, Style, and Technique

After you choose a format, you have a number of other decisions to make about your radio or television commercial. The format is only the large framework within which you will work. You also have to choose the structure (which may be determined by the format), the style, and the techniques you will use to enhance your selling message.

You do not, however, have to begin by choosing a format. Your commercial idea may well have been inspired by the punch line of a joke, an intriguing print ad, or the refrain from a popular song—in which case you could well begin with a style (humor), a technique (computer graphics), or a musical idea. The important goal is not to start at a particular stage in the creative process, but to start somewhere and then to consider all the formal, structural, stylistic, and technical options in a relatively systematic or orderly way.

Structure

A well-structured commercial—containing a logical sequence of related facts, impressions, and scenes—has a better chance of making its audience react favorably and profitably. Structure is the backbone of your sales message. It establishes continuity in the action and coherence among the parts. Rather than restricting a viewer's or

listener's understanding and interest, a unified structure, imaginatively conceived, actually helps him or her follow your logic or get involved in your story and remember your message.

In a continuing research study for an important TV advertiser, this fact stood out: Commercials with strong, well-defined structures registered much more powerfully than those with little or no design. The better-structured commercials were not only better remembered; they were also superior in influencing the decision to buy.

As stated in Chapter 3, some formats have their own unique structure, their own special way of arranging scenes or events. The problem-solution format requires a presentation of the problem followed by a presentation of the solution. In the slice-of-life commercial, the main character or characters move from a state of ignorance about the product, through a product test or trial, to a state of awareness of and satisfaction with the product. The narrative format follows a strict storytelling scheme. And the demonstration necessarily presents the product as it actually works in a step-by-step process.

The other formats—product alone, spokesperson, testimonial, and musical—usually focus on a single product feature or consumer benefit. When several features or benefits are treated, it is sometimes useful to proceed from least to most important, or vice versa.

In addition, any of these formats can use a structure ordinarily identified with a different format: problem-solution, ignorance-trial-awareness, story, or demonstration. However, the presenter-spokesperson-testifier discusses the problem and its solution, takes the audience through the discovery process, or tells a story of product use. The musical—uniquely—is adaptable to any structure, including demonstration, which can be performed by singers and dancers or animated figures.

Vignettes

Besides these standard structures, there are many other methods of arranging material in a radio or television commercial. "Vignettes" are a series of brief scenes in which the same action is performed or the same characters perform different actions. Diet Pepsi used a number of short glimpses of slim and attractive people, with musical accompaniment, to show the visible benefits offered by a low-calorie soft drink. Alka-Seltzer presented a series of close-up shots focusing on a variety of stomachs adversely affected by overeating and overdrinking. And True Value demonstrated the various ways in which its worktable could be used by do-it-yourself homeowners.

In these cases, the commercials consisted almost entirely of vignettes, with the product making an appearance either intermittently or at the end. However, the vignettes were—as they almost always are—used within a problem-solution, slice-of-life, or demonstration format.

This structure fits products that can be used in different ways, appeal to a variety of people, or rest on one very specific selling point that bears repeating. It seems to be most effective with a self-explanatory video, minimal voice-over, and a strong music track.

Comparison

When the product or service is demonstrably superior to, or at least different from, its competitors, a "comparison" might be in order. This structure can work three ways. First, you can show the "other" product or products and then show your own. Second, you can show the products performing side by side. Third, you can

show the products in a series of alternating scenes.

A variation of the side-by-side comparison is the head-to-head test, in which two competing products are tried by actors or actual consumers. Nabisco Shredded Wheat compared itself to three other breakfast cereals. Pepsi-Cola aired a series of commercials representing the results of a nationwide competition with Coca-Cola. Similarly, margarine has been tested against butter, and cars have been tested against each other for gas mileage and other features.

Continuing Series

The "continuing series" is a larger structural form in which the same characters or the same situation appears in one commercial after another. Like vignettes, the series usually focuses on one or, at most, two product attributes. It is particularly effective for "reminder" advertising—that is, when the product is well established and requires only the restatement of a simple campaign theme to sell the product. Probably, many continuing series are not planned for in advance but are developed as a result of one commercial's unusual success or because of the popularity of one or more of its characters.

Jerry Seinfeld for American Express, Jason Alexander for Rold-Gold pretzels, and Michael Richards for Diet Pepsi are examples of continuing presenters. A continuing series can also employ an actor playing a character, such as Ronald McDonald, Juan Valdez, or the Jolly Green Giant. It can be an animal, such as Morris the Cat, the Dreyfus lion, or the Merrill Lynch bull. It can even be imaginary, such as the Pillsbury Doughboy, Tony the Tiger for Kellogg's, or the Peanuts cartoon characters for Metropolitan Life.

Style

The word *style* derives from the Latin *stiles*, originally a writing instrument. Handwriting style is affected by the instrument you use and the way you use it. Commercial style means the way you present your material—how you hear it or see it and how you want it to be heard or seen. Style is a reflection of your perspective or point of view. Every commercial has a style. The goal is to make a choice from among the varieties of style and then to stick to it. Consistent style is as important as clear message and logical structure.

Comedy and Tragedy

The most obvious categories of style are the comic and the tragic. The latter is seldom used in radio and TV commercials because audiences tend to ignore or forget products or services that are associated with disturbing or depressing themes. They would rather be lifted up than let down. Of course, the difficulty is often unavoidable if the product or service deals with personal tragedy—death, fire, burglary, or disease. Thus, insurance companies, fire alarm manufacturers, security-system makers, and healthcare facilities must almost always take the risk. However, the tragic events inevitably portrayed, discussed, or at least mentioned are usually subsumed under the problem-solution format, and the final emphasis is on the solution that is available through purchase of the product or service.

Far more numerous are the radio and television spots that use humor in one way or another. In fact, many commercials are actually adaptations of standard stage, film, and TV comedy forms, such as comic sketches, situation comedies, standup monologues, and comic/straightman routines. And many of the spots that are not full-blown adaptations of established comedic forms use some kind of humor, including slapstick, puns, jokes, and comic characters.

Comic sketches are problem-solution or slice-of-life commercials in which one or more characters act out a more or less real-life situation that ends in a joke—often at the expense of the main character.

Situation comedies are commercials (usually slice of life) in which the same characters in the same comic situation appear again and again. The principal characters—Bill Cosby for Jell-O, the Maytag repairman, or the "Yes, I Am" impostor for Bud Light—ordinarily participate in variations of the same joke.

Standup monologues are often delivered by well known comedians, such as John Cleese, Judy Tenuda, and Jonathan Winters. The performer is often a spokesperson. But whether speaking for the product directly or promoting it indirectly by falling victim to the competitor's "shod-dy" product, he or she must bring distinctiveness to the role, usually by caricaturing a particular personality type. Straight-man/comic routines have been performed by James Garner and Mariette Hartley in a classic campaign for Polaroid, Ray Goulding and Bob Elliot for a variety of products, and comedy teams such as Stiller and Meara. Typically, one actor plays Don Quixote (idealistic, naive, or gullible), and the other plays Sancho Panza (realistic, sophisticated, or wary).

Humor can be crossed with fantasy, as in the animated Star-Kist spots with Charlie the Tuna and in a Fruit of the Loom men's underwear commercial that showed a group of men dressed up as different kinds of fruit. Humor can also be used with special effects. A classic IBM campaign starred a Charlie Chaplin look-alike, with the film run in fast motion to create the effect of a silent film and to suggest the frenetic activity required to run a business without the help of a computer. FedEx showed a series of fast-talking package senders who had used the "wrong" air-courier service and were trying to explain why their packages were late. The audio was speeded up so as to be almost unintelligible.

Satire is a special form of humor in which a play (*Romeo and Juliet, A Streetcar Named Desire,* a movie (*Gone with the Wind, Casablanca*), a personality (Humphrey Bogart, Fidel Castro), or an event (the first moon landing, Columbus's discovery of America) is mocked or parodied. Naturally, the object of the satire must be widely known, and the treatment must unequivocally relate the commercial to its source.

The problem is that besides a small number of Old Testament stories (Adam and Eve, Samson and Delilah, Jonah and the whale), four or five Shakespeare plays, and such familiar works of art as the Venus de Milo, the Mona Lisa, and Grant Wood's American Gothic, few literary or artistic creations will do. However, subliterary works—comic books (Superman, Batman, Wonder Woman), fairy tales, popular songs, blockbuster films (*Field of Dreams, Forrest Gump*), comic strips ("Doonesbury," "Peanuts"), and TV programs with exceptionally high ratings—are frequently used for satirical purposes.

A well-crafted comedy commercial can be a powerful selling medium. However, humor is not a universal panacea. First, it is too often used as an easy way out of an advertising dilemma that could have been better solved by the use of a different kind of treatment. The fact is, as we suggested earlier, some products are ill-suited to comedy. Second, even if the product or service is appropriate for this style, the selling idea must be well integrated into the commercial. Otherwise, the spot may be very entertaining, but not very successful. Third, the humor must be readily understandable. It cannot be based on a highbrow novel, a seldom-seen foreign film, or a local or regional personality or event. Fourth, the humor must be inoffensive. It cannot insult any member of the audience, particularly minority groups. And most advertisers avoid using persons, places, things, or even words that are regarded as sacred by a religious group (for example, a rabbi, the Vatican, prayer, the Koran, communion, "miracle"). And fifth, the humor must "wear" under constant repetition. Nothing is more boring than a joke one has heard before.

Fantasy and Documentary

Two other contrasting categories of style are fantasy and documentary. The latter, less often used, tries to create a slice-of-life atmosphere that suggests spontaneous, unrehearsed, and therefore "realistic" dialogue and/or action. Usually, a voice-over announcer describes the scene, which may be a demonstration of the product, a trial use, or a dramatization of a problem. This style can also be used for supermarket, on-the-street, or shopping mall interviews. When the product speaks for itself—when it is genuinely new or different, solves a serious problem, or performs an important task or function—the no-nonsense approach, without frills or fanfare, can be very effective. In other words, if the goal of the commercial is solely to inform, the documentary may be the best style in which to present it.

When the message is less definite or less earth-shaking—when you are dealing with a parity product that appeals to the senses—you might want to go to the other extreme: fantasy.

The successful Chanel No. 5 commercials used a surrealistic dream sequence to create a make-believe world. In such a world, the product can be made, grown, used, or consumed happily and contentedly.

Fantasy works because audiences have been conditioned to accept it since early childhood, a fact well noted by advertisers of children's products, such as presweetened cereal, toys, fast food, and video games. A fantasy ad can appeal to almost anyone because of its charm or warmth or humor. However, you must never lose sight of the selling proposition or the product. Even though you suspend a viewer's or listener's disbelief, your purpose is to idealize the product—not provide a temporary diversion.

Fantasy can be divided into four types: the imaginary, the far away, the futuristic, and the nostalgic. The imaginary includes almost all animated commercials (Green Giant vegetables, Keebler cookies, Star-Kist tuna) and spots in which animals talk or fantasy figures (leprechauns, witches, unicorns) appear.

The far away fantasy uses such settings as rural scenes, mountains, European cities, jungles, deserts, the Arctic, and any unfamiliar terrain or locale—especially when it is idealized or romanticized. In the "futuristic" style, the commercial may simply use a setting drawn from an imaginary future—inside an intergalactic space bus or in a 21st-century city. In a commercial that only ran once, Apple Computer introduced its Macintosh model in a spot based on George Orwell's futuristic novel, *1984*. In this controversial commercial (Did it sell or merely entertain?), a woman athlete ran through a seated throng of uniformed figures hypnotically gazing at "Big Brother" on a television screen. After the woman smashed the tube with a sledgehammer, the voice-over underscored the conventional-versus-revolutionary theme of the spot.

"Nostalgic" commercials use the past rather than the future. Thomas' English Muffins portrayed the London of a century ago. Pepperidge Farm used a horse-drawn delivery wagon and a grandfatherly delivery man, all in a turn-of-the-century setting, to sell its bakery products.

In addition, regardless of how it departs from the here and now, any fantasy commercial can be given a surrealistic treatment. In this style, images are distorted, idealized, or exaggerated—usually by camera tricks or with computer-generated graphics. Levi Strauss created a series of spots made up of computerized visuals that presented a gravity-defying landscape populated by levitating figures and objects. This dreamy, highly evocative campaign created an alluring fantasy world to which Levi's promised to provide easy entry.

Technique

By "technique" we mean not just "a method for accomplishing a desired aim," but a technical method that depends on the use of mechanical equipment. Techniques are necessary whenever you must simulate either the video or audio portion of a commercial. You may need special sound effects—cars crashing, waves roaring, or assembly lines humming—that require either on-location recording, which may be too costly, or a reasonable facsimile. Or you may want to show a process—food digesting, a headache disappearing, or grass growing—that cannot be filmed because it is either internal or invisible or cannot be shown in 30 seconds because it stretches out over a much longer period of time. In such cases, animation, special recording equipment, unusual camera angles or lenses, or computer controlled cameras may be useful.

Animation

Until very recently, the production technique that most completely liberated the imaginations of copywriters and art directors was animation. This is so because virtually anything can be made to happen in animated commercials. Ordinary-looking people can perform superhuman feats. Animals can sing and dance. And even inanimate objects can be given human attributes and abilities. As a result, many products have acquired animal spokespersons. Solutions to such problems as stained teeth, tired feet, and stuffy noses can be dramatized vividly and graphically. And characters (as well as objects) can be made to "perform" exactly to the specifications of writers, artists, and directors.

Animation in commercials has been influenced by every animated film maker from Walt Disney to Ralph Bakshi and by cartoonists from Charles Gould to Gary Trudeau. The technique can be used to create a cartoon story in the slice-of-life format, a package logo brought to life with highly stylized drawings, or an abstract design that underscores a selling theme or enhances the visual appeal of a product. Animation can be achieved by moving stills, in which still photographs are shot in different ways to achieve the effect of movement, or by stop motion, in which three-dimensional figures (Speedy Alka-Seltzer and the Pillsbury doughboy) are photographed one frame at a time to simulate movement. Otherwise, animation requires that each of the 24 frames per second be produced individually.

Animated commercials are popular because they are entertaining. That is simultaneously their strength and weakness. If you have real "news" to communicate—about price, quality, or availability—it is often best just to say so. Entertainment may be a distraction. Also, if your message is very personal, you may want to avoid this potentially charming but somewhat impersonalizing technique. It is difficult for viewers to identify with cartoon characters. If you need to attract attention, however, if your sales idea would be enhanced by an entertaining presentation, or if your target audience is very young, you might want to consider using animation.

Animation embraces more than cartoons, however. It can be used to show a complicated process simply and clearly. It also allows you to reveal how products work in ways or places that are unfilmable or unphotographable—that is, when their operation is microscopic, when they work inside the body, or when the problem they solve might be more tastefully presented symbolically rather than actually (for example, toilet bowl stains, body odor).

Yet again, because animation is expensive, it should be used carefully and selectively. If you need to demonstrate something that cannot be demonstrated in any other way, use animation. Or if you think the fantasy achievable through animation fits your product and message, use it. However, if you can do nearly as good a job without investing the extra time and money required by this technique, try something else.

Computer Graphics

Computer animation has broadened the horizons of advertising people far beyond the possibilities offered by the hand-drawn variety. In computer animation, the color and movement that otherwise require the drawing of every frame can be generated from one piece of black-and-white art. Each frame of film can be layered with any number of superimposed images. And three-dimensional objects can be moved, rotated, and distorted in any conceivable way. The result is a visually spectacular end-product in which images contract, expand, explode, implode, and undergo dazzling transformations that are impossible to achieve by other means.

Among the first successful computer commercials was a fantasy spot for 7UP that focused exclusively on a winged woman who floated above multicolored bubbles and amidst fountains of bright lights and other pyrotechniques. The visual drama created by this eye-catching and eye-holding scene was entirely sufficient to maintain viewer interest and involvement. Additional action or explanatory voice-over were completely unnecessary.

Another outstanding example of computer-generated effects is a TRW spot based on Martin Escher's optical illusion paintings in which objects are transformed into other objects through subtle gradations of form and color. In this commercial, a bird was shown to be part of an interlocking pattern of birds. In turn, the spaces between the birds became fish. And, from a more distant perspective, birds and fish were seen to be dots in a photograph of a man's face.

The same advantages and disadvantages apply to computer as to hand-drawn animation. On the one hand, it is an entertaining technique that can attract and hold interest. On the other hand, although it creates a more or less abstract or symbolic or "unreal" universe in which incredible things happen, it is also quite impersonal. And the temptation to achieve artistic perfection or show off technical virtuosity is almost as strong for advertisers as it is for writers, artists, and technicians. One way to solve the problem of impersonality is to combine computer graphics with live footage of real things and people, as NCR did in a spot featuring a revolving polyhedron with vignettes of company workers and products displayed on each geometrical facet of the turning globe. Used in the station-break logos of all the major networks, computer graphics seem to be especially good for corporate advertising in which an image of technological sophistication is the campaign theme.

Special Effects

In radio, special effects include all the simulated sounds that can be reproduced with real objects (for example, doors closing, shoes walking) and special recording equipment. In TV, special effects include all these, as well as simulated visual effects achieved by special cameras, unusual camera techniques, special processing equipment, and editing.

The purpose of special effects is to create an illusion. Backgrounds can be created by "rear projection," or projecting a moving or still picture on a translucent screen that gives the effect of a "real" set behind the actors and props. The illusion of a wild animal crashing through a wall (Schlitz), a 6-inch-tall man standing on a table at a restaurant (T.G.I. Friday's) or an animated character sitting on top of a real car (Rusty Jones) can be achieved by "matting," in which two different scenes are shot separately and later combined into one. Shots can be taken from different perspectives and combined. Objects can be miniaturized as models to create the effect of shipwreck, a flood, or a fire. Various lenses can be used to soften the focus, stretch the visual image, or otherwise distort the picture. Two or more different scenes can be shown on the screen at the same time ("split screen"). Product entrances and exits can be enhanced by fades (both in and out). Film can be speeded up ("fast motion"), slowed down ("slow motion"), reversed, or frozen. The possibilities are almost limitless.

Special effects are sometimes necessary and often useful, but they can, like other commercial enhancements, clutter up the listening or viewing experience or provide an easy, but unsatisfactory, way out of a tough communication problem. It cannot be said often enough that no technique should be used unless it dramatizes, clarifies, underscores, or in some way enhances the selling idea. After all, special effects are, as the name implies, special. They should not be employed unless they fulfill a special need or solve a special problem. To be used effectively, they must be chosen carefully and integrated smoothly into the commercial.

Exhibit 4–1. Integrating Elements: Lee

Advertiser: Lee Company
Agency: Fallon-McElligott
Product: Lee Jeans

Title: "Jeansercize"
Format: Demo/Burlesque/Music
Length: 30 seconds

(SFX: AEROBICS DANCE TRACK
THROUGHOUT)
LEADER: Alright everybody,

check the size.

Put one leg through.

Spin around. Lie on your back, kick
and pull.

Blow air through your hair and . . .

try it again and tug . . . and pull . . .

and stomp . . . and get real mad.

Take 'em off.

FVO: Considering what you go
through to put on most women's
jeans,

who needs an exercise program?

Try Lee.

The brand that fits.

Structure, Style, and Technique **41**

Exhibit 4–2. Integrating Elements: Connecticut General

Advertiser: Connecticut General Life Insurance Co.
Agency: Cunningham & Walsh, Inc.
Product: Estate planning

Title: "Sandcastle"
Format: Problem-Solution/SFX/Music
Length: 30 seconds

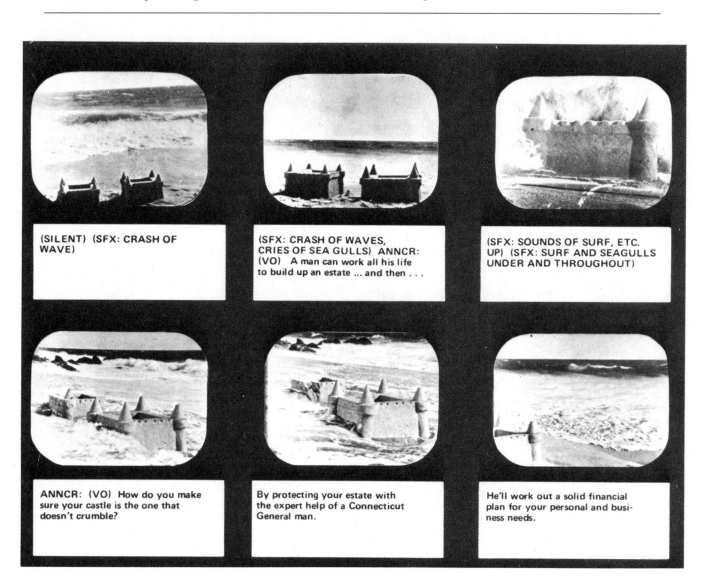

(SILENT) (SFX: CRASH OF WAVE)

(SFX: CRASH OF WAVES, CRIES OF SEA GULLS) ANNCR: (VO) A man can work all his life to build up an estate ... and then . . .

(SFX: SOUNDS OF SURF, ETC. UP) (SFX: SURF AND SEAGULLS UNDER AND THROUGHOUT)

ANNCR: (VO) How do you make sure your castle is the one that doesn't crumble?

By protecting your estate with the expert help of a Connecticut General man.

He'll work out a solid financial plan for your personal and business needs.

And he'll give it the time it deserves, so it'll stand up.

You know something?

On the average a CG man prepares just five plans a month.

That's why his plan stands up.

See a Connecticut General man ... before the next tide comes in.

(MUSIC) At Connecticut General, ...

we do things a little differently.

(MUSIC)

Connecticut General Life Insurance Company.

Exhibit 4–3. Integrating Elements: Mocap

Advertiser: Mobil Chemical Co.

Agency: The Martin Agency

Product: Mocap nematicide-insecticide

Title: "Insects"

Format: Spokesperson/SFX

Length: 30 seconds

ANNCR:	If you could hear the insects that eat your corn, you'd start using Mocap nematicide-insecticide as soon as possible. If you could hear the rootworms . . .
SFX:	ROARING
ANNCR:	wireworms . . .
SFX:	SCREECHING
ANNCR:	nematodes . . .
SFX:	HISSING
ANNCR:	and black cutworms.
SFX:	CRUNCHING
ANNCR:	If you could hear the worms robbing you of forty bushels of corn or more per acre . . . If you could hear the cutworms cutting your good, healthy stalks off at the base . . .
SFX:	TIMBER FALLING
ANNCR:	If only you could hear it . . .
SFX:	SILENCE
ANNCR:	But you can't. So you may be sitting back using no insecticide at all. Hoping the worms won't do too much damage this year. Or maybe you're using an insecticide that doesn't protect against all four of these deadly pests. We repeat: If you could hear the rootworms, wireworms, nematodes, and black cutworms, you'd be using Mocap—the only insecticide in America that protects against all four. Because you're in the business to save corn. And so is Mocap. Mocap. Get it.
SFX:	ROARING
ANNCR:	And save the corn.

Section Two

Radio Commercials

5

An Overview of Radio Advertising

The first radio commercial was broadcast by New York's WEAF in 1922, two years after the first regular radio programming began on stations KDKA in Pittsburgh and WWJ in Detroit. The advertiser, a tenant-owned apartment complex in Queens, paid $40 for a 15-minute day-time program on the advantages of suburban living. Ironically, the first radio commercial was actually an "infomercial"—that is, the kind of in-depth advertisement that eventually disappeared from radio because of increasing costs and has returned to use via cable television within the last decade.

Two years later, National Carbide Co. became the first network advertiser. In 1926, Wheaties aired the first singing commercial. And in 1931, A&P broke through the almost decade-long ban on mentioning product features in radio spots. The company was permitted to tell listeners how much its products cost.

Besides the industry's periodic revision of its codes governing program content (the first was established in 1929 by the National Association of Broadcasters) and its various attempts to find a reliable way to measure the size of radio audiences (beginning in 1930), the most important developments in the medium, at least as far as advertisers are concerned, were 1) the establishment of commercial FM stations in 1941, 2) the first network purchase of radio programs in 1948 (they were originally developed and owned by advertisers and agencies), and 3) radio's recovery of its television watching audience in the 1950s (which was aided by radical changes in programming formats).

Radio Today

The same year that first radio commercial aired, Herbert Hoover, later President of the United States and then, as Secretary of Commerce, responsible for administering the Radio Act of 1912, commented on the astonishing increase in the number of radio owners and in the size of the radio audience: "We have witnessed in the last four or five months one of the most astounding things that has come under my observation...today, over 600,000 persons possess wireless telephone receiving sets, whereas there were less than 50,000 such sets a year ago."

If he were alive today, Mr. Hoover would undoubtedly be even more astounded to know that there are more than two radios for every person in America. According to the Radio Advertising Bureau (RAB), the average U.S. household has 5.5 radios. Every year, people buy 10 million more radios. Ninety-five percent of all cars have radios.

In 1923, there were 573 radio stations in the country. In 1992, there were 4,961 AM and 4,785 FM stations, for a total of 9,746.

The increase in the number of special-interest stations has had a profound effect on the listening habits of the American consumer. RAB statistics indicate that radio reaches 96.5 percent of all Americans each week. Arbitron rating service listenership figures show that Americans listen to radio for 2 hours and 39 minutes per day and more than 18½ hours per week. Advertisers know that commercial messages can be delivered to listeners no matter where they are. Researchers have found that 44.4 percent of all people tune in to radio at home, 27.3 percent listen in cars, and 28.3 percent are potential customers elsewhere—at work, in stores, at the beach, in parks, and even on sidewalks.

Radio's invasion of the streets has been aided by the popularity of battery-powered sets, including both large portables and walk-along, miniature receivers equipped with earphones and used by joggers and mass transit riders. Over 38 million walk-along sets are now in use. All age groups enjoy personal portables: teens age 12 to 17 (33.5 percent), adults age 18 to 34 (43 percent), and adults 35 or over (23.5 percent). Thus, far from dying when television entered the scene, radio has benefited from its own technological advances and has taken on a prosperous life of its own.

Back in the 1950's, after the first devastating impact of television had subsided, radio transformed itself. It turned to more modest programming and to many small advertisers to make up the revenue it had lost. It began to feature what had been its filler material, using news and music as its staples and seeking regional and local, rather than national, advertisers. Through foresight, flexibility, and innovation, radio revitalized itself and became a prime medium for advertisers, large and small.

Radio Advertising

In 1992, radio advertising exceeded 8.7 billion dollars annually, a 5 billion increase since 1980.

People listen to radio primarily for information, news, talk, entertainment, and sports. Nearly 95 percent of the population 12 years of age or older listen to some radio broadcasts every day. And from early morning to the start of prime evening time, more people listen to radio than watch television. Interestingly, the RAB reports that more than 50 percent of the adult population rate radio as a release from loneliness and boredom. It is a very personal medium for advertisers.

Important, too, is the fact that radio is an intimate, friendly medium. Disc jockeys, open mike hosts, and local commentators attract and hold audiences today as did the network personalities of the golden age of radio when "Fibber McGee and Molly," "Amos 'n' Andy," and Jack Benny were tune-in musts.

In addition, radio early established an amazing believability. Orson Welles's famous 1938 broadcast, based on H.G. Wells's *War of the Worlds*, "visualized" an invasion from Mars that frightened millions of listeners and moved thousands to flee from their homes in terror. As Mr. Welles said at a radio workshop, "Oh, we knew that radio, used inventively, could glue the listener to his overstuffed Morris chair, get him involved, and make him believe. But we never dreamed to what extent."

Radio is personal, friendly, and believable. Anyone attempting to write effective commercials should take advantage of these attributes. Advertisers, large or local, wisely include radio in their marketing mix. Accounts with even modest national budgets can work wonders with radio alone. One jams and jellies company, Smucker's, used radio extensively with a unique creative approach to establish its name nationally. Most supermarket brands sold for a few cents less than Smucker's, so radio spots had to give consumers the idea of high quality. This goal was accomplished with a mildly self-deprecatory "recall trap." Every spot used this reminder "With a name like Smucker's, it has to be good." Listeners across the country could identify this line, readily recall the brand name, and play back the quality message.

Many other advertisers have used radio extensively, if not exclusively. General Mills, which found success with heavy spot radio campaigns for Nature Valley Granola and Granola Bars, Breakfast Squares, and Golden Grahams, boosted its radio spending from zero to more than $7 million. The biggest spender in the medium, Sears Roebuck, spent over $100 million annually in the early 1990s. Competitors Montgomery Ward, J.C. Penny, and K Mart also used radio extensively. In the same period, General Motors and Chrysler were major radio advertisers. So were AT&T, MCI, PepsiCo, and Procter & Gamble. The reason? The medium works. Midas International, after adding radio to its usual television schedule, credited that mix with boosting sales 30 percent in one year.

Such success is not automatic, however. People seldom just sit and listen to radio attentively. They are busy doing other things while their radios are turned on. More perhaps than with any other advertising medium, the basics of attention, interest, involvement, and conviction must be achieved in each radio commercial.

Radio has also made great strides in audience measurement. Gone is the idea of homes listening to radio, for homes do not listen. People listen. The old research technologies did not keep up with the multiplicity of radio sets around the house, in the car, and at the office. The old mechanical gadgetry underestimated radio's audience. So the industry—the Radio Advertising Bureau and the National Association of Broadcasters combined—undertook the All Radio Methodology Study (ARMS I) to determine which methods of audience measurement might provide station owners and advertisers with an accurate determination of their listeners.

As a result, better ways of counting audiences were invented. Advertisers on radio now have a much better idea of what their dollars deliver. Along with local market studies by ARB, Pulse, Mediastat, Hooper, The Source, and others, a national measurement was developed. The national networks cooperated to create their own study to replace the old Nielsen national homes listening research that depended on meters too large to be attached to all the sets in a household.

Advantages of Radio Advertising

Radio was expected to die out as an advertising medium when television entered the scene. It did not. Radio revenues did dip drastically, but broadcasters examined the medium for its strengths, fed and exercised them, and came up with new programming—and commercial health. Today, radio is a potent selling tool for

good reasons. The five following advantages stand out.

1. *Radio is ubiquitous.* Nearly half a billion radios are in working order. Of these, 73 percent are in homes, stores, barbershops, and offices. Cars and truck account for well over 100 million of them. And portable radios by the scores of millions are toted just about everywhere—even to sporting events that are being broadcast play by play. Furthermore, unlike the print media, radio cannot be ignored. If you are within hearing range of a turned-on radio, you will hear it whether you want to or not.

2. *Radio is selective.* The geographic, demographic, and programming diversity of radio stations helps media buyers pinpoint their target audiences. Such flexibility means that your spots can be read by a live announcer on local stations. Or they can be broadcast on regional or national networks. They can be aired at just about any hour of the day or night.

Advertisers can choose from a variety of AM or FM stations, each with a distinctive format: all news, adult contemporary, country, black, oldies, top forty, beautiful music, middle of the road (MOR), classical, talk, ethnic, or foreign language. Such diversity allows the copywriter to "speak" directly to prospects.

3. *Radio is economical.* In a single week, radio reaches nine out of ten people 12 years of age and over. Those 18 and older listen for nearly three and a half hours a day. An advertiser can usually count on an effective combination of reach and frequency for a relatively low cost per thousand listeners. Alone or in a mix with other media, radio can effectively help stretch ad budgets. Spots can be scheduled for as few or as many plays as objectives and budget dictate.

Another economy: Radio commercials are relatively inexpensive to produce, ranging from no cost, when a script or ad-lib fact sheet is used by a live/local announcer, to a modestly budgeted full production with music, sound effects, and talent.

4. *Radio is fast.* If the need arises, an advertiser can have a live/local commercial on the air within hours. Spots using sound effects, music or jingle, and several voices can be rehearsed, recorded, mixed, dubbed, and then played on

the air within days. This is a break for advertisers who must meet occasional emergencies, such as an air-conditioner dealer whose territory is suddenly smothered by a heat wave.

5. *Radio is participatory*. Along with a sense of friendliness and loyalty to a particular station, listeners, develop a sense of involvement. Radio calls the imagination into play. Commercial "stories" are unrestricted as to place or time. Sound effects and music instantly establish a scene. Description or dialogue can be as vivid as taste allows, and characters can be played either straight or as comic caricatures. The listener uses imagination to fill in the "color" and details. For instance, a spot for a pub-style restaurant featured King Arthur and his knights galloping in for dinner. There were no horses, of course, just sound effects and actors in a studio.

Any or all of these characteristics of radio can be used to advantage by creative advertisers and agencies to prepare and present commercials that sell.

Guidelines for Radio Advertising

A review of the successes and failures in radio advertising over the last 50 years has generated the following list of do's and don'ts. Consider these suggestions in deciding what will work best for your radio spot.

1. *Write for the ear*. Write conversationally. Forget that there may be thousands of people listening to your message. Write as if you are talking to one person. And be sure to make your commercial visually and conceptually clear through words and sounds.

2. *Capture and excite the listener's imagination*. By using only sound, your spot must perform effectively in the "theater of the mind." With the competition your product (and your commercial) faces, you can't afford to be dull, pedantic, or prosaic.

3. *Stick to one strong idea*. Concentrate on one main persuasive thrust. You can add an extra copy point or two, but do it with care. Too many messages confuse. Also, unless you are far and

away the market leader, do not sell generically for the whole product category: sell your product's benefits.

4. *Single out your prospect*. If you have done your research, you know who buys your product and why. Keep your target consumer in mind when you write your commercial. If your product alleviates backache, do not start by describing June roses. Get right to the point: "If you suffer the agony of a sore back...." Your talent selection can help. A company making skin care products featured a nationally famous disc jockey talking to teenagers about acne. Because of his involvement with popular music, he was a listened-to authority figure, and he successfully reached the intended audience.

5. *Set the mood for your product*. How fast should your commercial be delivered? What tone of voice should your "homemaker" employ? Is the music too "busy" for your product's image? These and a dozen other questions should come to mind when you write a commercial. Your answers will determine the "tone" or approach. To get the right one, you must be conscious of how you want the listener to hear—and react.

After deciding on tone, write directions in your script as to how you wish each line to be read ("angry," "happy," "sad," "irritated," and so on). A spokesperson picking up your script should have specific directions. When you indicate the kind of delivery you want, everyone benefits.

It's worth repeating: Radio can do just about anything, from a straightforward, news-oriented sales pitch to a wildly imaginative satire. But you must be careful not to get carried away. The commercial's tone should match the product's image: they should be compatible.

6. *Remember your mnemonics*. Be sure to set a memory trap—and spring it. It might be in the copy, the music, the sound effects, or a combination of them, but it must be meaningful. If you can use a distinctive and memorable sound—the "hummmmmmm" of a Mazda engine or the "Mm-mm good!" response of a child eating Campbell's soup—use it. Diet Pepsi zipped up a zipper and Alka Seltzer plopped and fizzed.

7. *Get attention fast*. The first five or six seconds in a radio commercial are vitally important.

If you fail here, the whole spot may be a wasted effort. An automotive product began a commercial with an announcer speaking over a public-address system at a race course: "Gentlemen, start your engines!" And immediately afterward a roar of engines was heard. Expend a lot of creative thought on your opening.

8. **Register the product's name.** Some copy chiefs might add, "Early and often!" Because you do not have the use of headlines, as you do in print advertising, or even a shot of the actual product, as in television, you must establish the product name by repeating it during the spot.

A commercial for Guv'nor, a restaurant in Manhattan, featured a conversation between and English tourist and a native New Yorker. The tourist began with, "I say, guv'nor, can you recommend a good restaurant?" The New Yorker replied, "Sure…Guv'nor." The Englishman responded, "Jolly good, guv'nor, now if you'd just tell me the *name* of this restaurant." And so it went, the two people never quite communicating, the listener enjoying it, and the restaurant name being repeated many times.

9. **Don't overwrite.** Don't crowd your spot with too much copy. Like "white space" in print ads, silence (for at least a second or two) can help focus attention on your main message. Use easy-to-understand words, and keep phrases and sentences on the short side. Write in the present tense and active voice as much as possible.

Read your commercial aloud or have someone read it to you. Change any words that interrupt continuity or are difficult to pronounce. Allow for announcer breathing (and listener hearing) time. Word count varies with approach, delivery, mood, and so on, but the following figures are generally accepted averages for straight announcements.

10 seconds: 20–25 words
20 seconds: 40–45 words
30 seconds: 60–70 words
60 seconds: 150–180 words

If you find your copy running beyond these limits, make sure that it can be read within the allotted time, or rewrite it.

10. **Make your appeal clear.** There are few basic human needs (shelter, food, clothing, and love), but human wants seem unlimited. So you have a wide choice when it comes to selecting and crafting a persuasive appeal. A good question to ask is: "What want or need does this product satisfy?"

You can use logic if your product is a hard-nosed performer and you can explain why it works so well. If it saves either time or money, you should say so. But don't stop there. Go beyond cold logic into the warmer currents of emotional persuasion. Time saved can become extra time for your consumer to do other things, and money saved can be spent for other fulfillments.

11. **If it's news, make it sound important.** First make sure that what you have to say is news. Too many commercials promising news have made customers wary. So if you are writing about the semiannual white sale at the local department store, do not treat it as an earth-shaking event.

However, if the facts are important, repeat them again and again. Treat significantly lower prices, genuinely new products, and spectacular promotions the way they deserve to be treated—with the radio equivalent of big headlines and exclamatory copy.

12. **Multiply your TV impressions.** If the audio track for your television spot can double—that is, serve as a radio commercial as well—it stretches the ad dollar nicely. When a listener hears a spot he or she has seen on TV, it can be instantly visualized, at no extra cost to the advertiser.

13. **Keep a friendly feeling going.** Engage your audience, but do not irritate or anger. Remember, you are trying to win friends, as well as influence prospective customers and retain present buyers. How many grumpy salespeople are successful? And the point applies to the entire commercial, not just the lead-in. Make it smile!

14. **Be sure that your humorous spots are funny.** Why does almost every copywriter begin by thinking that the way to sell is to be funny? Not every product is amenable to humorous treatment. And not every listener has a similar sense of humor. For these reasons, many ostensibly funny commercials do not sell. Worse yet, many that seem amusing to copywriters may not be so perceived by clients and audiences.

15. *Give the listener something to do.* The bid for action, usually near the end of the commercial, is like a salesperson's request for an order. What do you want the listener to do? Where? When? If it's a local spot, use an address and ask listeners to drop in. Immediate action demands a phone number. If the commercial is national, close with your strong selling theme. This gives the listener a final opportunity to react to—and commit to memory—your main appeal.

16. *Once is not enough.* If you mention a telephone number, be sure to repeat it. Keep in mind that the listener is not glued to the radio, breathlessly awaiting your sales pitch. Chances are, he or she will not have pencil and pad at the ready. Give everyone a chance to record essential information, including address and even store hours. Your spot may be spectacular, but if customers don't know where to go or whom to call in order to get the product, you have lost sales and wasted your valuable time.

6

Examples of Successful Radio Commercials

National Radio Commercials

This chapter contains examples of successful network radio commercials. In fact, some of the spots actually helped to reverse a decline in sales, and a few turned a big loss into a comfortable profit.

Note how the spots embody the formats discussed in Chapter 3. Pay special attention to the way sound effects, dialogue, and/or music are integrated. Note how different elements are used with different formats and different products. Although the commercials shown here differ in format, style, and technique—as well as marketing objective and target audience—they are all attention-getting and persuasive.

For each spot, we have provided the names of the advertiser, the agency (when available), and the product or service; the type of format; and the length. In addition, the final four spots have analyses affixed to the scripts. Can you add anything else to these analyses? What can be said about the first four?

Note the manner in which these scripts are laid out. The left side of the page, typed in capital letters, indicates who is speaking and whether and when music and sound effects (SFX) are to be used. The right side, typed in both upper and lower case letters, presents all the copy that is to be read. In addition, special instructions and directions concerning music and sound effects are given in caps. Sound effects are frequently underlined with a broken line, and music directions are sometimes underlined with a solid line.

Local Radio Commercials

Local spots are often made on short order with severe financial limitations. For that reason, the ads on the following pages are valuable as examples of the high quality of work that can be created within tight constraints. Pay particular attention to the economy of effect achieved in those ads, which are lacking in musical accompaniment, special effects, and/or other production "extras."

The most effective solution to the budget/deadline crunch is, in most cases, use of the spokesperson format. The following examples—almost all of which are straight announcements—should be analyzed in terms of how they present product features and benefits. Some local radio spots confine themselves to only one feature or benefit. However, most emphasize more, including—most often—price, quality, variety, and convenience.

When you examine these commercials, note whether they are delivered in first (we), second (you), or third person (they). Also note sentence length, word choice, and use of sentence fragments. Do they close with an express or implied bid for action? Do they register the store or product name? For each spot, try to imagine what kind of voice and delivery would work best.

Exhibits 6–9 to 6–14 give examples of spots created for, and aired in local markets.

Exhibit 6-1. National Radio: Airtouch Cellular

Advertiser: Airtouch

Agency: Bozell/SMS

Product: Cellular phone

Title: "Mogul to Lumis—VP of Coffee" Starter

Format: Burlesque/Slice-of-Life

Length: 60 seconds

Script

SFX:	PHONE RING - PICK UP
LUMIS:	Hello?
MOGUL:	Lloyd B. Lumis?
LUMIS:	Uh huh...
MOGUL:	J.J. Mogul here, of Mogul Pictures.
LUMIS:	Uh huh...
MOGUL:	Your screenplay needs a little work. Do you have your Airtouch cellular phone yet?
LUMIS:	Hey, I'm a waiter. I can't afford a cellular phone.
MOGUL:	Nonsense! Everybody can afford...oh look!
SFX:	POURING COFFEE
MOGUL:	Here's my VP in charge of coffee, uh, communications (WHISPERS TO KID) Tell him about Airtouch!
KID:	Well, uh, for $1.22 a day I got a brand new Airtouch portable and Airtouch service with their starter kit.
LUMIS:	Wow! $1.22 a day?
KID:	Yeah. You also get 20 minutes of cellular airtime a month at no extra charge.
LUMIS:	Even I can afford that!
KID:	Well sure you can. Just call 1–800–AIRTOUCH, and ask for their Airtouch starter kit.

LUMIS: Isn't there some kind of legal mumbo-jumbo?

KID: Ah, you mean—"Phone installed with purchase on approved credit, 24 equal payments of $7.25, 0% APR, one year service commitment required, roaming charges are not included, other conditions and restrictions apply, limited time offer, good in greater L.A. only"?

MOGUL: Is that it?

KID: Uh huh.

MOGUL: Good job. You're fired.

KID: More coffee?

MOGUL: Lumis; one thing. We ran your script through our research people...

LUMIS: Uh oh...

MOGUL: They loved it!

LUMIS: Wow!

MOGUL: 'Cept for two things.

LUMIS: Uh huh?

MOGUL: Lose the vampire...

LUMIS: Yeah...

MOGUL: Lose the cheerleader.

LUMIS: Thought so...

MOGUL: So call 1–800–AIRTOUCH, get that phone and stay in touch.

LUMIS: I'll stay in Airtouch.

MOGUL: I love the way you write...

ANNCR: Airtouch. The company that's making cellular service affordable.

Exhibit 6–2. National Radio: Pepsi

Advertiser: PepsiCo

Agency: BBDO

Product: Diet Pepsi

Title: "Burger with Everything"

Format: Burlesque/Slice-of-Life

Length: 60 seconds

Script

SFX:	THREE GUYS COME INTO A DINER, AT A BOOTH
WAITRESS:	Hi, guys.
GUY 1:	Hi.
GUY 2:	Hello.
GUY 3:	Hey.
WAITRESS:	You're my first customers.
GUYS:	Ahuh.
WAITRESS:	What would you like?
GUY 1:	Diet Pepsi.
GUY 2:	Same.
GUY 3:	Diet Pepsi me, lotta ice.
WAITRESS:	Three Diet Pepsi's...
GUY 1:	And I'll have a hamburger with everything.
GUY 2:	Cheeseburger, rare.
GUY 3:	Grilled cheese.
WAITRESS:	Okay...you want a Diet Pepsi and a cheeseburger with grilled cheese on it?
GUY 2:	No. *Cheeseburger*, rare.
WAITRESS:	Rare cheese?

GUY 2:   No, hamburger's rare, then cheese.

WAITRESS: You said, "Hamburger with everything."

GUY 1:   I said everything.

WAITRESS: "Everything" including cheese?

GUY 1:   No.

WAITRESS: No cheese on the hamburger?

GUY 2:   Cheese on *my* hamburger.

GUY 3:   And a grilled cheese.

WAITRESS: On *your* hamburger?

GUY 3:   No hamburger, just cheese.

WAITRESS: Then it wouldn't be a cheeseburger...?

GUY 2:   Let's start from the top: 3 Diet Pepsi's...

WAITRESS: Ahuh...

GUY 1:   Then make three cheeseburgers...

WAITRESS: Ahuh...

GUY 1:   Take the cheese off one, and put everything on it...

WAITRESS: 'kay...

GUY 2:   Take the second cheeseburger, and leave the cheese on it...

WAITRESS: 'kay.

GUY 3:   Take the third cheeseburger, take the burger off, and grill what's left...got it?

WAITRESS: That's it?

ALL GUYS: And three Diet Pepsi's.

ANNCR:	Every Diet Pepsi has freshness dating. So no matter how long it takes you to get your Diet Pepsi, you can be sure you'll get the freshest taste.
WAITRESS:	Okay, one hamburger with everything, one cheeseburger, rare, and one grilled cheese.
GUY 1:	She got it!
GUY 2:	Now, where's our Diet Pepsi's?
WAITRESS:	What Diet Pepsi's??
ANNCR:	Freshness Dating from Diet Pepsi. Nothing else is a Pepsi.

Exhibit 6–3. National Radio: Miller Lite

Advertiser: Miller Lite Brewing Co. **Title:** "Heaven or…"

Agency: Leo Burnett **Format:** Burlesque/Slice-of-Life

Product: Miller Lite **Length:** 60 seconds

Script

SFX:	WALKING TOUR, DOORS OPEN, FOOTSTEPS, SOUNDS FROM WITHIN, ETHEREAL MUSIC
MAN:	Here's your 75-inch big screen TV…
GUY:	Wow!
MAN:	Rec Room in there, hot tub, sauna and spa in there…
GUY:	Cool!
MAN:	And here in the 5 car garage, your convertible, your motor home, your 4 by 4 off-road vehicle, your limousine, and your dirt bike.
GUY:	This is incredible! Does everybody come here?
MAN:	Just the lucky ones. And for tonight, which concert and/or championship sporting event would you like front row tickets for?
GUY:	Let me think about it. Oh, here's my new kitchen. Let's check the fridge!
MAN:	All stocked with beer!
GUY:	Yeah…but there's no Miller Lite!
MAN:	Oh, there's no Miller Lite anywhere around here, and won't be for all eternity.
GUY:	But without the great taste of an ice cold Miller Lite how can you call this place "Heaven"? (ALT. LINE: But with the great taste of an ice cold Miller Lite, Life is Good. You thought of everything else, how come you didn't think of Miller Lite here in Heaven?)
MAN:	What makes you think this is…HEAVEN? HA HA HA HA!!!!!!

SFX:	"COMING OUT OF A DREAM" HARP GLISSANDO
WOMAN:	Honey, wake up. You're having a nightmare!
GUY:	Wha...? Where am I? More importantly, what's in the fridge?
WOMAN:	You're home in bed, and the fridge has yesterday's meat loaf...
GUY:	Yes?
WOMAN:	Some potato salad...
GUY:	Yes??
WOMAN:	And a 6 pack of Miller Lite.
GUY:	OH YES!!! Life is Good!
TAG:	Miller Lite Brewing Company, Milwaukee, Wisconsin.

Exhibit 6-4. National Radio: Full View TV

Advertiser: General Instruments

Agency: Phillips Ramsey

Product: Full View TV

Title: "Changing Announcer"

Format: Announcer/Comedy

Length: 45/15 seconds

Script

Introducing Full View TV. What is Full View TV? Maybe this will help. Think of me as the voice of 350 channels, up in the sky just waiting for you to get them.

(TURNS TO A SPORTSCASTER, DICK VITALE TYPE) Sports channels with all your favorite sports...

(NOW BECOMES A SMOOTH POWERFUL MOVIE TRAILER ANNCR) Premium channels with your favorite movies and entertainment...

(STAND UP COMIC TYPE) But seriously, Folks, comedy channels...

(NEWSCASTER LIKE C.N.N.) And in other news, news channels...

(ENGLISH P.B.S. TYPE) Indeed, educational and cultural programming options...

(SUPER KID) Music channels of all kinds, Dude...

(ACTRESS FROM 1940s MELODRAMA) Oh, Charles, don't forget our love and all the classic movie channels...

(OBNOXIOUS OVER-THE-TOP SPORTS ANNCR) Plus live coverage of ground-pounding, fire-breathing Monnnsterrr TTTRRUUCCKKSSSS!!!

(JULIA CHILDS TYPE) As well as tips on how to serve a delicious dinner for 12...

(KID) And kid stuff for kids...

(BACK TO REGULAR ANNOUNCER VOICE) Full View TV brings to you all the television there is to bring. Not only regular TV, but cool behind-the-scenes stuff and "wild, unannounced" sports feeds no one else even gets. Full View TV gives you more television entertainment than any other system. Full View TV. From General Instruments. It's the Ultimate Satellite TV.

Exhibit 6-5. National Radio: *Operation Dumbo Drop*

Advertiser: The Walt Disney Co.   **Title:** "Buying a Ticket"
Agency: Buena Vista Pictures   **Format:** Burlesque/Slice-of-Life
Product: *Operation Dumbo Drop*   **Length:** 55 seconds

Script

SFX:	MULTI-PLEX TICKET OFFICE
DAD:	Let's see, I'd like five tickets to see *The Happiest Puppy*.
WOMAN:	No you don't.
DAD:	Yes I do.
WOMAN:	No, you don't.
DAD:	Aren't you just supposed to be selling me tickets?
WOMAN:	Is that your family there?
DAD:	That's right.
WOMAN:	Are you telling me they don't want to see a movie where an elephant skydives out of an airplane?
DAD:	'Scuse me? Could you say that again?
WOMAN:	Disney's *Operation Dumbo Drop*. The movie where an elephant sails on a boat.
DAD:	You said he dives out of a plane?
WOMAN:	He does.
DAD:	An elephant?
WOMAN:	He also hitches a ride on a truck.
DAD:	The same elephant that dives out of a plane?
WOMAN:	The very same.
DAD:	A real elephant?
WOMAN:	Very real.

DAD: When the elephant jumps out of the plane does he...does he...you
                know...

WOMAN: Hey—it's a Disney movie, okay?

DAD: Say no more. Five tickets to *Operation Dumbo Drop*. And thanks for
                the tip.

WOMAN: Next?

KID: Yeah, I'd like two tickets for *Night of the Atomic Chainsaw
                Massacre, Part 7*.

WOMAN: No you don't...

KID: Yes I do!

WOMAN: No you don't!

TAG: Disney's *Operation Dumbo Drop*. Rated PG, parental guidance
                suggested.

Exhibit 6-6. National Radio: Call Waiting

Advertiser: Sprint/United Telephone
Agency: Agnew & Corrigan Advertising
Product: Call Waiting

Title: "Bob"
Format: Slice-of-Life
Length: 60 seconds

SFX:	Phone ring, pick up
BOB:	Hello?
BOSS:	Johnson? This is Mr. Wembley.
BOB:	(Obsequiously) Oh, hello, Sir. How are you?
BOSS:	Get down to the office now and finish that monthly report.
BOB:	But, Mr. Wembley, Sir, it's Saturday and I'm taking the kids to...
BOSS:	Oh, who cares...
BOB:	...the zoo.
BOSS:	...Johnson! You just get your little behind down to the...
SFX:	Beep, beep
BOSS:	What's that?
BOB:	My Call Waiting, Sir. It means I have another call. I'll be right back, Sir, I promise. (Click, Click) Hello?
WOMAN:	Bob Johnson?
BOB:	Yes.
WOMAN:	Hi Bob, sorry to call you on a Saturday, but I've decided to offer you that position we talked about. And at the salary you requested.
BOB:	Terrific! I can start Monday.
WOMAN:	Oh wonderful. See you then.
BOB:	Bye. (Click, Click) Mr. Wembley?
BOSS:	Yes.

<u>BOB:</u>	I do not work on Saturday, fatso!
<u>BOSS:</u>	Fatso!?
<u>BOB:</u>	Why don't you finish that report all by yourself!
<u>BOSS:</u>	Me!?
<u>BOB:</u>	Yeah, between doughnuts. And by the way, we all know it's a toupee...
<u>BOSS:</u>	It's not a toupee! It's a hair hat.
<u>BOB:</u>	It's a toupee, and a bad one, Sir.
<u>BOSS:</u>	No, it keeps me warm, you see...
<u>BOB:</u>	Bad toupee.
<u>ANNCR:</u>	With Call Waiting from Sprint/United Telephone, you'll never miss another call, even if you're on the line with someone else. Call us at 1-800-767-9878 and get call waiting from Sprint/United Telephone. Who knows what you might be missing?

Exhibit 6–7. National Radio: Red Lobster

Advertiser: Red Lobster Inns

Agency: D'Arcy-MacManus & Masius

Product: Spiced shrimp dinner

Title: "AM Drive Time/Shrimp"

Format: Testimonial/Musical

Length: 60 seconds

Script

SINGERS:	HOW DO YOU LIKE YOUR SHRIMP, WE KNOW HOW YOU LIKE YOUR SHRIMP! RED LOBSTER FOR THE SEAFOOD...
JOEL:	And shrimp!
SINGERS:	LOVER IN YOU!
JOEL:	You know, usually I don't make any dinner plans while I'm driving to work in the morning...but one has to be flexible...and the idea of sitting down to a half pound of spiced shrimp at Red Lobster tonight, well it sounds delicious. Think of it...a half pound of shrimp cooked up in a spicy blend of seasonings...you just peel 'em, pop 'em in your mouth and ahhhhh. Ready for another one? There you go, ohhhh...hot...hot. How 'bout a shrimp dinner at Red Lobster tonight? Be strong now...wait till dinner...ah about eight hours from now...oh make that seven hours fifty nine minutes & 12 seconds...You can do it...
SINGERS:	HOW DO YOU LIKE YOUR SHRIMP, WE KNOW HOW YOU LIKE YOUR SHRIMP! RED LOBSTER FOR THE SEAFOOD...
JOEL:	It'll give you something to look forward to!
SINGERS:	LOVER IN YOU!
RECORDED TAG:	Spiced Shrimp are something deliciously new at Red Lobster. Come in and try 'em tonight!

Analysis: The Red Lobster jingle, made familiar to both radio and TV audiences by frequent repetition, served as a readily identifiable company signature. Although the jingle remained the same in every commercial, each spot in the continuing series featured a different Red Lobster specialty. Note that the testifier is cast in the role of his audience, people driving to work. And his appeal is directly, dramatically, to the senses.

Exhibit 6–8. National Radio: WICO

Advertiser: WICO Corp.

Agency: Bentley, Barnes & Lynn, Inc.

Product: WICO joysticks

Title: "Whacko over WICO"

Format: Spokesman/Slice-of-life/Musical

Length: 60 seconds

Script

SONG:	YOUR STICKO WON'T GO WHACKO WHEN IT'S A WICO. (REPEAT)
ANNCR:	WICO won't go whacko because it's the only authentic arcade joystick you can use at home. Over 500 arcade video games use WICO controls. The most durable, the most accurate...the fastest controls money can buy.
BOY:	Wow! I'm scoring at home like I've never scored. I'm whacko over WICO.
SONG:	YOUR STICKO WON'T GO WHACKO WHEN IT'S A WICO.
TEEN BOY:	They're as tough as the joysticks at the arcade.
TEEN GIRL:	He's whacko over WICO.
MOM:	I've been practicing.
DAD:	She's whacko over WICO.
ANNCR:	There are more WICO joysticks than you can shake a stick at. Command Control Joysticks, Computer Control Joysticks, and the new BOSS that lets you boss any game around.
SONG:	YOUR STICKO WON'T GO WHACKO WHEN IT'S A WICO. (REPEAT)

Analysis: The memorable jingle frames the sketch in this excellent mixed format spot. The spokesman, providing specific product information, speaks after the opening and before the closing song. And, in between, three members of the family convey their enthusiasm for the product, while two others give added punch to the testimony.

Exhibit 6–9. Local Spot: Las Vegas

Advertiser: Las Vegas

Agency: Eribrit Productions

Product: Las Vegas

Title: "Las Overwhelmos"

Format: Burlesque/Slice-of-Life

Length: 60 seconds

Script

CLIENT: Run that by me again?

GUY: Our ad agency feels Las Vegas should change its name.

CLIENT: But, it's always been Las Vegas. It's on all the maps.

GAL: Our focus groups found the name Las Vegas was…too vague.

CLIENT: Vague?

GUY: Las Vegas is all different now. Full of fun for everyone.

CLIENT: People know to come to Las Vegas for fun.

GAL: But they may not realize how much fun.

GUY: Las Vegas. Does that say anything about the new pyramids? "Egyptville" would be more accurate.

CLIENT: But Las Vegas is on all our ashtrays…

GAL: Well, how about the pirate ship? Las Vegas could become "Aaaarrrsdale!" with a little eyepatch over the "r."

CLIENT: Las Vegas is on over 62-thousand swizzle sticks…

GUY: Las Vegas…does that say volcano? Bengal tigers? Diving dolphins? We think "Las Overwhelmos" is more like it!!

CLIENT: And all those little guest soaps…?

GAL: Excitementown!

GUY: Funburg!!

CLIENT: I know Las Vegas has super-collassal new family attractions and non-stop entertainment…but we're not changing Las Vegas' name and that's final!

GUY: Okay, allright! Here's a little something we've done for lots of our other ad accounts...*New and Improved* Las Vegas!

GAL: In the convenient economy pack.

GUY: (FADING) Plenty of free lighted parking.

GAL: 32, count 'em 32 attractions...

GUY: Shop and save...

CLIENT: Okay, okay. I get it. Lemme think about it...

ANNCR: There's never been a better time to visit Las Vegas, a world of entertainment in one amazing place. Brought to you by the Las Vegas Convention and Visitors Authority.

Exhibit 6–10. Local Radio: Frontier Certainty

Advertiser: Frontier Communications   **Title:** "Certainty"
Agency: Rumrill-Hoyt   **Format:** Burlesque/Slice-of-Life
Product: Frontier Certainty   **Length:** 60 seconds

SFX:	(TELEPHONE RINGING; SOMEONE PICKING IT UP.)
BUSINESSMAN:	Hello?
SFX:	(BLAH, BLAH?)
BUSINESSMAN:	This is he.
SFX:	(BLAH, BLAH, BLAH)
BUSINESSMAN:	No, I do not sit around thinking about my long distance rates—I have Frontier Certainty.
SFX:	(BLAH, BLAH, BLAH, BLAH, BLAH)
BUSINESSMAN:	Now wait a minute, lemme get this straight. It's 14 cents a minute for the first five minutes, after which it will be 25% off every other minute for six months but only in states beginning with the letter T?
SFX:	(BLAH, BLAH, BLAH)
BUSINESSMAN:	Uh, no thanks.
SFX:	(BLAH, BLAH, BLAH!)
BUSINESSMAN:	No—really. Thanks, but like I said, I've already got Frontier Certainty.
KAREN VO:	Introducing Frontier Certainty. Every month, we show you, right on your statement, what you'd be charged on the top six plans from AT&T, MCI and Sprint. You pay whatever's lowest. That's it. Frontier Certainty. Exclusively for Frontier business customers. Call 777-2000 for details. And then, when those other guys call, you just tell them "Uh-uh, certainly not."

SFX: (BLAH, BLAH, BLAH?)

BUSINESSMAN: No, I will not switch even if you do throw in a spillproof travel
                  mug.

Exhibit 6–11. Local Spot: Rockwell Drivetrain Plus

Advertiser: Rockwell

Agency: Bozell/Detroit

Product: Rockwell Drivetrain Plus

Title: "Sappleman's Salsa" RV2

Format: Burlesque/Slice-of-Life

Length: 60 seconds

Script

BOSS:	Well, Darlene, today's the big day. We ship our first batch of Sappleman's Super Salsa.
SECRETARY:	Have you talked to Shapiro in shipping?
BOSS:	Why?
SECRETARY:	That big onion shipment never came in. One of your trucks broke down...
BOSS:	Oh no...
SECRETARY:	I tried to tell you about Drivetrain Plus from Rockwell, sir...
BOSS:	Drivetrain Plus?
SECRETARY:	It's from Rockwell, so trucks stay on the road.
BOSS:	Well, let's not panic. I guess Sappleman's Super Salsa doesn't need onions.
SECRETARY:	Or tomatoes, either...
BOSS:	Tomato truck broke down too?
SECRETARY:	I must have showed you that Rockwell Drivetrain Plus brochure at least ten times, sir...
BOSS:	So...we'll be the first salsa that's nothing but jalapeno peppers, water, and salt.
SECRETARY:	Sir...?
BOSS:	The jalapeno pepper truck?
SECRETARY:	Why not just call the Rockwell Customer Service Center right now at 800-535-5560 and get their information on Drivetrain Plus?
BOSS:	(Near Tears) All those glass jars filled with nothing but water and salt...

SECRETARY: Paper bags, sir.

BOSS: You mean the truck with the glass jars...

SECRETARY: Here's the phone, sir.

TAG: Drivetrain Plus by Rockwell—The Industry's Most Complete
Drivetrain! Call 1-800-535-5560.

Exhibit 6–12. Local Spot: Perkins Restaurants

Advertiser: Perkins Family Restaurants

Agency: Direct

Product: Perkins Restaurants

Title: "Showdown"

Format: Burlesque/Slice-of-Life

Length: 60 seconds

Script

MUSIC:	SPAGHETTI WESTERN STYLE THEME
SFX:	SPURS JANGLE DOWN A LONELY WESTERN STREET
SLIM:	Okay, Jake, you lily-livered varmint, I'm callin' you out.
JAKE:	You want a gun fight, Slim, you got it—you horn-swogglin' horny toad.
SLIM:	Tomorrow at dawn. Just you 'n' me.
JAKE:	Fine. I'll be...I'm sorry, did you say "dawn"?
SLIM:	That's right.
JAKE:	Oh. See, tomorrow at dawn I was gonna go to Perkins Family Restaurant for their special Steak and Eggs breakfast.
SLIM:	Oh, you were, were ya?
JAKE:	Yeah! So let's make it high noon, okay?
SLIM:	Well, gee, that's when I was gonna go to Perkins for their new Steak and Eggs Special. How about sundown?
JAKE:	No can do. I'm takin' the school marm to Perkins.
SLIM:	Well, how's tomorrow A-M look for you?
JAKE:	Let me check my book. (FLIP, FLIP) Dentist at 11. Afternoon?
SLIM:	Sorry, I'm coachin' Little League...
ANNOUNCER:	Try either one of Perkins two great Steak and Eggs specials at an extra-special price. The 7-ounce sirloin steak with 2 eggs, hash browns, plus 3 famous Perkins pancakes for just 4.99 (5.99)(5.99)(7.99) or Perkins 9-ounce strip, plus the same for only 6.99 (7.49)(7.99)(9.99). Both served anytime, all the time.

SLIM: Tell you what; let's meet at Perkins and we'll work it out.

JAKE: Okay, I'm pencillin' this in. "Perkins...Steak and Eggs with Slim to re-sched gunfight tomorrow morning..."

SLIM: Late morning! That way I can still make my aerobics class...

ANNOUNCER: Offer good at participating Perkins Family Restaurants for a limited time. Perkins. Breakfast, Dinner and Everything In Between.

Exhibit 6–13. Local Spot: Rheingold

Advertiser: C. Schmidt & Sons, Inc.   **Title:** "Supermarket"

Agency: John Emmerling   **Format:** Slice-of-Life

Product: Rheingold beer   **Length:** 60 seconds

Script

MUSIC:	STOCK—STRIDENT, PATRIOTIC
ANNCR:	New York is learning that Rheingold...the extra dry beer with a stout, creamy head that stands up longer than Schaefer, Miller, and even the expensive import Heineken...that Rheingold is now out to beat inflation. Here now, a typical checkout counter...
MUSIC/SFX:	MUSIC FADES INTO BABBLE OF SUPERMARKET SOUNDS
WOMAN CHECKER (CHEWING GUM):	Asparagus...
SFX:	CASH REGISTER SOUND
CHECKER:	$3.29...Chuck roast
SFX:	CASH REGISTER SOUND
CHECKER:	$6.50...Rheingold beer...Wait a minute! This price is marked wrong! It's too low!
MAN:	Yeah, listen...I'm in a hurry. I just want to...
CHECKER:	Hold on, honey! Beer prices are up all over town...
MAN (QUIETLY FURTIVE):	Well, maybe you could let the Rheingold slip through this time...
CHECKER (BECOMING INDIGNANT):	This is America, fella! Raising prices is practically patriotic! Manager! Manager to checkout six!
MANAGER (DEEP VOICE):	Okay, what's the trouble here?
MAN:	Well, nothing really...

CHECKER:	This guy is trying to buy Rheingold at the wrong price.
MANAGER:	Frieda, Rheingold is out to beat inflation. That's the right price.
CHECKER (TO HERSELF):	That's the right price? (TO CUSTOMER) Oh, sir, I owe you an apology...
MAN:	Yeah...I'll settle for the beer.
MUSIC:	STRIDENT, PATRIOTIC THEME
ANNCR:	And so, fellow New Yorkers, check the price of the beer you drink—then check Rheingold. Try the premium quality that beats inflation. Rheingold!

Analysis: It's not easy to combine music, sound effects, humor, and dialogue into an effective and comprehensive commercial. This one does it so forcefully that it actually turned sales around in a matter of weeks. Although this spot deals with a problem (inflation) and a solution (inexpensive beer), it does not follow the problem-solution format. The slice-of-life scene takes place in a supermarket and is played out by three "average" characters.

Exhibit 6–14. Local Spot: Magee's

Advertiser: Magee's Clothing
Agency: Ayres & Associates, Inc.
Product: Jeans

Title: "Jeans, Not Rock"
Format: Slice-of-life/Musical
Length: 60 seconds

Script

MUSIC:	ESTABLISH LIGHT ROCK RHYTHM, KEEP UNDER DIALOGUE
MAN:	Hey, Magee's Stone Woman, you still making history?
WOMAN:	I sure hope not.
MAN:	Listen, Stone Lady, we're worried about your super-cool costume. The winters here are very whippy, and we think your little dinosaur dress is going to give you leg cramps. How about if we turn your teeny dress into a *top* and put it over some new jeans from Magee's Junior Girls?
WOMAN:	You trying to change my style?
MAN:	Now don't get paranoid?
WOMAN:	Para...what?
MAN:	Paranoid. Means clever as a chicken. Many of Magee's new jeans have a gold underwear stitch around the powderhorn pockets and down the side...
WOMAN:	Talk *rock*!
MAN:	Can't. I don't know how. Some have buttons, some zip fronts, some high-rise, some wide waistbands, some wide legs...
WOMAN:	Talk *rock*!
MAN:	I can't, Stone Woman. I don't understand your crazy rock talk. Now many of Magee's junior-girl jeans are by Prophet and Friends...
WOMAN:	...rock music!
MAN:	Nah, the Prophet and Friends group makes *jeans*, not music... course, you could wear 'em to rock around the campfire on cold nights...

WOMAN: Aha! *That's* rock talk. Your cave or mine?

JINGLE: HEY, WHEN YOU WANNA BE WHAT YOU WANNA BE,
                WHY DON'T YOU COME AND SEE MAGEE'S.
                SEE MAGEE'S, LINCOLN AND OMAHA,
                SEE MAGEE'S.

MUSIC: END

Analysis: Notice how this commercial reaches for its special audience—junior girls—with an imaginary Stone Age character. One of a continuing series, this spot gets to the product easily and quickly, then uses the time-honored technique of a dialogue in which one character doesn't seem to understand what the other (who usually gives the sales pitch) is talking about. This technique keeps the subject alive and developing and the copy points coming until the final fillip. The jingle serves as a strong reminder as well as a bid for action.

7

Radio Assignments

This chapter contains assignments that give you an opportunity to exercise what you have learned about radio advertising. Before you begin to write, review the advice about writing commercials in Chapter 2, the discussion of formats and other elements in Chapters 3 and 4, and the guidelines for writing radio spots in Chapter 5. Give yourself time to think. And choose the components of your commercial with the product, consumer, and competition in mind. If you get stuck, review the sample radio scripts in Chapter 6 for ideas and alternatives.

Some of the assignments ask you to work with background data or with a brief summary of marketing objectives. In some instances, you will be requested to rewrite a radio, TV, or print ad—without benefit of product or market information other than what appears in the ad. In all cases, you should prepare a creative strategy statement (see Exhibits 1-1 and 1-2) based on the data available. Don't contradict the facts as they are given, but feel free to fill in the blanks when necessary. After you have written a strategy statement, study it carefully. Use it as a point of departure and keep checking it as you write to make certain that you are staying on target.

Unless your instructor tells you to do otherwise, follow the script style shown in the exhibits at the end of Chapter 6. That is, for every assignment, name the advertiser, indicate which format(s) you are using, name the product or service, and give the length of the commercial. In writing the script, use capital letters for titles or names of speakers, sound effects, music cues and copy, and stage directions. Double space all assignments. Photocopy blank radio script sheets when necessary.

Assignment 7-1: Background Data

THE CLIENT: Pet Paradise

THE PRODUCT: A full line of pet foods (seeds and pellets) for birds and small animals (gerbils, hamsters, rabbits, and so on). Each food is scientifically formulated to provide optimum nutrition and dietary balance for each kind of animal.

THE MARKET: Pet owners, animal breeders, and pet store owners (to feed the animals in their stores).

THE PACKAGE: Each food in the line is available in four packages: a 14 ounce box (4" × 8" × 2") and 5-, 25-, and 50-pound bags. All have identical coloration—salmon pink with dark-green type. The product name (GERBIL FOOD, FINCH FOOD, and so on) is spread across the middle of the package. A green palm leaf logo follows the "PET PARADISE" name on the bottom third.

DISTRIBUTION: Supermarkets (boxes), pet shops, and discount chains (both boxes and bags).

PRICE: Same as its major competitor, the largest pet food distributor in the nation.

AD BUDGET: $1,500,000 annually.

MARKETING PROBLEM: Lack of consumer awareness has led to brand erosion.

1. Write a 60-second slice-of-life spot using sound effects.

2. Write a 30-second spinoff in any format.

Radio Script Sheet

Student name: **Advertiser:**
Date submitted: **Product:**
Commercial length: **Format:**

Assignment 7–2: Background Data

THE CLIENT: Claussen's Catfish

THE PRODUCT: Claussen's catfish are carefully raised in fresh well-water ponds, or farms. They are fed a special formula of selected grains and grain products. This raising method produces a catfish light in color, flakier in texture, and more delicately flavored than ordinary catfish. (Some people compare it to Dover sole.) These fish are high in protein and low in cholesterol, calories, and fat. They are always sold fresh as uniform-sized whole fish, steaks, and fillets.

THE MARKET: The fish is purchased mostly by women, but it is eaten by people of both sexes and of all ages. The best geographical market is in the South and along the Mississippi River, where catfish are more commonly eaten. Claussen's catfish is popular with dieters.

THE PACKAGE: All cuts are sold in random weights in light blue foam trays that are sealed in a clear poly wrap. Red diagonal printing—running from the upper right-hand corner to the lower left-hand corner—includes the words "CLAUSSEN'S CATFISH," "FRESH," and "FARM-RAISED." Cooking suggestions are printed in black on the lower right portion of the wrapper. The company logo is two "Cs" linked together.

DISTRIBUTION: Nationwide in supermarkets, seafood shops, food brokers, institutional and restaurant suppliers.

PRICE: $4.99 per pound, comparable to trout and other better-quality fish.

AD BUDGET: $250,000 annually.

MARKETING PROBLEM: Lack of trial has caused sluggish sales.

1. Write a 60-second testimonial without sound effects or music.

2. Write a 30-second musical that includes a jingle.

Radio Script Sheet

Student name: **Advertiser:**

Date submitted: **Product:**

Commercial length: **Format:**

THE CLIENT: A-One Brake Service

THE PRODUCT: This independent service station offers complete repair service on all foreign and domestic cars, including brakes, front end, tires, transmissions, and exhaust systems. Six experienced mechanics are trained to do everything, from tune-up and lubrication to body work and painting. Service is fast and dependable. Prices are fair, and the owner, who has been at the same location 20 years, is friendly and accessible.

THE MARKET: A-One's main customers are business people and other white-collar workers who drive to their downtown offices and park their cars within a ten-block radius of the A-One shop. Competition includes one franchised dealer whose station does not offer a full line of car services and a run-down independent station that offers inexpensive but dependable work.

THE PACKAGE: A-One is an efficiently run operation. Mechanics wear uniforms, and the shop is kept as clean as possible.

DISTRIBUTION: The downtown area of Big Bluff, Illinois, population 140,000.

PRICE: All service and repair prices are competitive, but lower than those at the franchised shop and higher than those at the other privately owned station.

AD BUDGET: $15,000 annually.

MARKETING PROBLEM: Business at A-One Brake Service has declined because of a few well-publicized consumer complaints about the physical condition of the shop before its recent refurbishing.

1. Write a 60-second straight spokesperson announcement with sound effects.

2. Write a 30-second spinoff without embellishments.

Radio Script Sheet

Student name: **Advertiser:**

Date submitted: **Product:**

Commercial length: **Format:**

THE CLIENT: Miller & Webb

THE PRODUCT: Miller & Webb men's clothing store has made a special purchase of 1,500 dress shirts. The manufacturer of the high-quality shirts, a nationally known advertiser, has given Miller & Webb a special price in order to reduce surplus stock. The shirts are current styles in a variety of solid colors and stripes. All have long sleeves and two-button cuffs. The fabric is "no iron" broadcloth of 65 percent polyester and 35 percent cotton.

THE MARKET: Men, 18 years old and over. Competitors can offer equal quality but not comparable prices.

THE PACKAGE: The shirts will bear the national advertiser's label. Miller & Webb is an upscale men's shop located in a suburban Atlanta shopping mall.

DISTRIBUTION: Miller & Webb's mall outlet.

PRICE: $25.00 each.

AD BUDGET: $5,000 in radio for this promotion.

MARKETING PROBLEM: Consumers are unaware of the store's offer of high-quality merchandise at low prices.

1. Write a 60-second spot in the spokesperson format using one of the store owners.

2. Write a 30-second straight announcement delivered by a paid spokesperson.

Radio Script Sheet

Student name:	**Advertiser:**
Date submitted:	**Product:**
Commercial length:	**Format:**

MARKETING: For many years a life insurance company, Prudential has extended its coverage to property and casualty. The marketing goal is to create an awareness among adults that Prudential agents can provide automobile and homeowner as well as life insurance through Prudential's new property and casualty divisions.

ADVERTISING: Prudential wishes to announce its new business and familiarize the public with the name of its new divisions: Prudential Property and Casualty Insurance Co. The advertising should also state that the company may be able to save the consumer money on car and home insurance. Present life-insurance policy holders can deal with their current agent. And potential buyers can now take care of all their insurance needs at Prudential. The long-standing theme of the company's advertising has been "Own a piece of the rock." The corporate logo is a circle enclosing an illustration of the Rock of Gibraltar.

1. Write a 60-second commercial in the slice-of-life format.

2. Write a 30-second spinoff in any format.

Radio Script Sheet

Student name: **Advertiser:**

Date submitted: **Product:**

Commercial length: **Format:**

Assignment 7-6: Marketing Objectives

MARKETING: A large and successful food manufacturing company has decided to market a new product called Sweet 'n Tart cranberry sauce. The marketing objective is to achieve year-round sales. Traditionally, cranberry sauce has only been used on holidays such as Thanksgiving and Christmas.

ADVERTISING: The campaign should make consumers think of serving cranberry sauce throughout the year. The association with Thanksgiving and turkey should be avoided. The product should be associated with other holidays or seasons and with a variety of foods, ranging from ham and cold cuts to steak and lamb chops.

1. Write a 60-second spot in any format using any combination of special elements.

2. Write a 30-second spinoff.

Radio Script Sheet

Student name: **Advertiser:**

Date submitted: **Product:**

Commercial length: **Format:**

Assignment 7-7: Fact Sheet

Many advertisers take advantage of the skills of local DJs and/or announcers who are particularly adept at ad-libbing. Rather than restrict them to following a script, they are given fact sheets about the product or service. It is then up to each announcer to provide a lead-in, lace the different sales points together, provide persuasive word-pictures, and end with a strong call to action. The fact sheet below, prepared for the Australian Trade Commission, supplies the names, description, and uses for the products to be sold in an extemporaneous spot.

PRODUCTS: Australian apples and pears.

- A fresh supply of Australian apples and pears has just arrived.
- Two varieties of pears are Bosc and Parkhams ("Park-ums").
- Both are sweet and succulent and have a distinctive taste.
- They may look like domestic pears, but their taste is superior—their flesh is white and aromatic.
- Pears shipped to the United States are the best of a vintage crop.
- The apples are called "Granny Smith" apples.
- Green in color, they are nevertheless magnificent eating apples.
- These apples can also be used in cooking.
- Now available in grocery stores and supermarkets at a price about the same as domestic apples and pears.
- More and more people are asking for them, so hurry—before they are sold out.

1. Write a 30-second commercial in the spokesperson format.
2. Write a 30-second spot in another format.

Radio Script Sheet

Student name: **Advertiser:**

Date submitted: **Product:**

Commercial length: **Format:**

Assignment 7–8: Rewrite

This radio commercial used an actual disaster as the basis for a compelling message: Despite a fire that destroyed the agency's offices and equipment, the company was still in business. While the spokesperson format worked well, the "good news" could have been communicated in other ways. First read the script and then do the assignments below.

1. Write a 60-second revision of this commercial in a spokesperson/interview format.

2. Write a 60-second problem-solution commercial using sound effects.

ANNCR:

This is a message to the people who burned down our office building the day before Christmas. Contrary to reports in the media, Martin/Williams Advertising was not one of seven businesses destroyed by the fire you set. You burned our offices, you burned our furniture, you burned our equipment, and you burned a lot of valuable personal things. But you didn't put us out of business. Two days after you set the fire we found temporary office space...slightly worn, but usable. Three days after you set the fire we salvaged all our financial records, all our media records, most of our art files...we moved them into our new space. Four days after the fire, including a day off for Christmas, we were hard at work producing advertising for our clients. We don't know why you set the fire. Whatever your motivation, we're pretty burned up about it. But we're not burned out. We're still open for business, still actively seeking new business. Martin/Williams Advertising. Temporarily located at 909 Hennepin Avenue in the Pence Building. Right next door to the fireproof hotel.

Radio Script Sheet

Student name: **Advertiser:**

Date submitted: **Product:**

Commercial length: **Format:**

Assignment 7–9: Rewrite

The following carefully written and effectively delivered 30-second spot worked its magic without music, dramatic story, or sound effects. With a deep, resonant voice, the spokesperson successfully communicated the "ferocity" of the product by emphasizing the words "kills" and "croak." Examine the script and then revise it according to the directions below.

1. Write a 30-second revision of this spot in a problem-solution format. Add special effects.

2. Write a 30-second version in any other format.

ANNCR:

In the beginning there was soap and water...then came medicated cleanser. And now there's Oxy Wash with 10 percent benzoyl peroxide...it actually helps prevent pimples. While Oxy Wash gently washes away dirt and oil, its benzoyl peroxide kills acne bacteria with a ferocity unequaled in modern face washing. Want to help prevent tomorrow's pimples today? Then don't just soak your acne bacteria, croak them.... Wash with Oxy Wash.

Radio Script Sheet

Student name: **Advertiser:**

Date submitted: **Product:**

Commercial length: **Format:**

The TV script below was created to introduce a new, exclusive style of Mott's apple sauce, Golden Delicious Chunky. It was also used in certain markets as a wedge to gain distribution of other Mott's styles. The advertising was intended to show consumers that Mott's makes the style of apple sauce they like—and makes it better. Read the script carefully and then rewrite it as directed.

1. Rewrite this TV spot as a 30-second testimonial for radio.

2. Rewrite it as a 30-second musical.

VIDEO	AUDIO
BOY STANDING NEXT TO TABLE WITH FOUR JARS OF MOTT'S ON IT. HE TAKES INTRODUCTORY BOW.	
BOY FACES CAMERA.	BOY: Apple sauce by Mott's...the best apple sauce in the whole world is made by Mott's.
ECU OF JAR AND BOWL.	There's Mott's regular...
ECU OF HIM TASTING.	(SILENCE AS HE TASTES)
BOY WITH ECU OF JAR AND BOWL.	and Cinnamon...
ECU OF BOY TASTING.	(SILENCE AS HE TASTES)
BOY WITH ECU OF JAR AND BOWL.	Cinnamon Flavored Country Style...
ECU OF BOY TASTING.	(SILENCE AS HE TASTES)
BOY WITH ECU OF JAR AND BOWL.	and a new one...Golden Delicious.
BOY TASTING.	WOMAN (VO): Very good, Tommy...new Mott's Golden Delicious Chunky with little chunks of golden delicious apple.
HIS NAME IS SUPERED.	BOY: And you thought Mott's just made regular apple sauce...

Radio Script Sheet

Student name: **Advertiser:**

Date submitted: **Product:**

Commercial length: **Format:**

This half-page print ad is dominated by the headline. Illustration and copy are kept to a minimum. Staying with the primary selling theme, revise the ad for use on radio according to the directions given below.

1. Write a 30-second spot in the slice-of-life format.

2. Write a 30-second commercial in the problem-solution format.

TAKE THE SHOCK OUT OF YOUR ELECTRIC BILL.

Introducing the new Frigidaire Frost-Proof Refrigerators.

The most energy efficient refrigerators we've ever made.

In fact, our Frost-Proof line is the most energy efficient line of frost free refrigerators in the industry.

So efficient they start saving you money on your electric bill the minute you plug one in.

Savings that grow day after day. Month after month. Year after year.

FRIGIDAIRE
HERE TODAY, HERE TOMORROW

Radio Script Sheet

Student name: **Advertiser:**

Date submitted: **Product:**

Commercial length: **Format:**

Section Three

Television Commercials

8

An Overview of Television Advertising

As funny as it now seems, the purchase of a TV set was once surrounded with the kind of excitement and hoopla generally reserved for such major events as the birth of a child, or the announcement of a marriage proposal. The "buzz" about the new medium was immediate and widespread: TV combined the broadcasting power of radio and the appeal of movies, and promised to bring already popular forms of entertainment—vaudeville, live theater, and films—into everyone's living room. For free!

The initial excitement notwithstanding, the influence television would have, not only here, but worldwide, was vastly underestimated. Television has affected lives and lifestyles of the American people more than any other innovation in mass communications except the printing press. And it is probably at least equal in cultural impact to those other wonders of the 20th century—the airplane, the automobile, and the computer.

Since its birth in the early 1940s television has proven to be an almost unparalleled vehicle for popular culture, entertaining vast audiences around-the-clock with an ever-increasing menu of musical, dramatic, and comic performances. But TV has provided more than entertainment. Television has made instant and extensive news coverage and analysis part of the daily and nightly diet of millions of viewers through regularly scheduled morning and evening news programs.

It brought the Gulf War, the O.J. Simpson trial, and the Oklahoma City bombing into the homes of Americans—daily, graphically, and powerfully. And it transformed the political process by making it almost mandatory for candidates for national office to appear, speak, and debate before the penetrating eye of the TV camera.

Attendance at movie theaters plummeted drastically in the 1950s as a direct result of TV's growing popularity. Small-town inhabitants abandoned Main Street on weekend nights for television's then modest fare. And families everywhere, it is said, gave up conversation in exchange for a few hours of silence in front of the television screen.

Even TV commercials have become an important part of American culture. It is not unusual for network news program to "turn the camera" on commercials, and then frequently provide grist for radio talk shows, newspaper articles, and magazine feature stories. This is particularly true in the political arena, where advertising campaigns of competing candidates receive an almost disproportionate amount of public scrutiny.

Television Today

At the start of the 1950s, fewer than one in ten American households had a television set. Ten years later, set penetration approached the 90 percent level. Today, 99 percent of all U.S. homes have color sets. Over 66 percent have more than two sets. According to A.C. Nielsen statistics, the average American watches television more than ever, 7 hours and 17 minutes a day. To meet this demand, America had 1,505 TV stations and 11,461 cable TV systems as of 1993.

Commercial television is not, however, without its problems. Probably the most important challenge it faces is the decline in its share of viewership brought about by the growth and development of cable television and its limitless variations. This loss began in 1980 and continued as more and more cable choices became available. The cable networks have something unique to offer: specialized programming aimed at specific, though smaller, audiences. Over 59 million homes, 63 percent of all households, receive cable. In 1995, there were close to 50 advertiser-supported cable networks. The number will surely increase.

Some experts predict that television will change more in the next ten years than it has in the previous 50. New technologies—microwave facilities, Satellite Master Antenna (SMATV), Direct Broadcast Satellite (DBS), and High Definition TV (HDTV)—will become available. Monitors will become "smart," and may combine some of the functions of other high-tech devices. For instance, the "TV-computer" might monitor other household appliances or store movies in memory, the "TV-telephone" could make video conferencing possible. And the "TV-printer" may deliver store coupons while commercials are in progress. Or the TV set of the future may do all this, and more. Fiber optics and new compression technologies will allow for up to 500 channels and interactive programming and commercials.

Television Advertising

Many people question the psychological and cultural effects of television. However, few can deny that, for better or worse, television has transformed American life, especially the consumer marketplace. Television reaches big numbers of people with big impact at big costs. And it involves big risks and equally big rewards. In 1993, the average national spot cost $222,000 to pro-

duce. A commercial for Alamo Rent A Car that ran during the 1994 Super Bowl cost $1 million to produce—and $3 million to air! Every year, Procter and Gamble spends well in excess of one billion dollars on TV media.

Of course, to be fair, you must compare the advertising costs of television to the costs of other media. For example, a full-page, 4-color ad in *Reader's Digest*, with a circulation of 15 million, costs over $166,000. In fact, although the costs of creating, producing, and airing a TV commercial are staggering, television is one of the most cost-efficient media. And when you factor in the impact of a TV spot—as compared to that of a radio commercial or a magazine ad—it becomes clear that no other medium lets you reach and influence so many people at so little cost per person. For about four or five dollars, you can have a personal salesperson call on a thousand potential customers, show them your product, demonstrate its effectiveness, and ask for an order. This advertising power has built brands that were unheard of before the advent of TV into national leaders, including Crest, Certs, and Clorets. Small wonder that considerable care and expertise should be given the preparation of every commercial.

Advertising on cable TV will become increasingly important as new research techniques enable advertisers to find out the size of the audience and its demographic and psychographic composition. It appears that cable TV will become a "magazine stand" of the air. Because each cable TV channel caters to a highly segmented audience with specific wants and needs, commercials have to be written to address these segments.

Advantages of Television Advertising

Television offers advertisers several distinct advantages over other media. Its most outstanding attribute, which no other medium can match, is its ability to reach vast numbers of consumers at the same time. Other advantages are impact, credibility, selectivity, and flexibility.

Television is powerful. TV has the strengths of all major media. Like direct mail, it comes directly to the consumer—into the home. Like radio, it offers sound, including special effects as well as music. And like print, it can show the product alone, in a setting, or in use. Furthermore, unlike any other advertising vehicle, television can portray the product in motion—whether it is poured, driven, eaten, worn, or otherwise consumed. The viewer sees the product in "real life," which means that TV can present its sales message far more forcefully than any other medium.

Television is believable. Although some viewers regard TV advertising as exaggerated and misleading, the medium has an undeniable capacity to induce belief because, as the old saying goes, seeing is believing. Viewers can actually see product users succeed where they have formerly failed, smile with satisfaction, and receive the visible and tangible rewards of success—praise, gratitude, and approval.

Furthermore, products can be demonstrated. Viewers can be shown how they work, what they do, and why they should be purchased. Advertisers can demonstrate how products perform in comparison with other products. And they can show products undergoing tests that prove their claim for effectiveness, strength, or durability. Other media can only report the results, not display them and thereby subject them to public scrutiny and judgement.

Television is selective. TV can reach any target audience—any age group and any demographic segment. Commercials aimed at children can be spotted on after-school programs; those directed at homemakers can be shown with daytime talk shows or dramas; and adult male viewers can be reached at night through commercials on sports shows. Spot TV allows both the national chain store and the national advertiser to advertise in markets in which a store or product needs extra support or in which potential sales are greatest.

Television is flexible. Advertisers can purchase time on TV locally, regionally, or nationally. Thus, television can be used by both local and national companies. Small, independent retailers can use local TV production facilities at comparatively low cost. And national advertisers can broadcast their selling messages from coast to coast or in selected local markets.

Guidelines for Creating a TV Commercial

Creating a TV commercial calls many skills into play: the playwright's way with words, the artist's eye, the director's touch, the psychologist's understanding of human motivation, and the salesperson's ability to convince. Any one of these might tend to overbalance the others, so add your sense of judgement to obtain the proper mix.

Your aim is to create a TV commercial with a powerful selling idea developed with imagination and presented with unity, coherence, and structure. To help you reach this goal, we have provided some general guidelines. They should serve to keep you aware of the medium's strengths and limitations and of the important target—the TV viewer you hope to reach, attract, and convince.

1. *Do your basic research first.* Get the facts—all the facts you can—about the product or service you are to advertise. Do not neglect either the competition or the consumer. Make sure you know what you are up against and whom you are trying to reach.

2. *Emphasize your main selling point.* Analyze your research and then crystallize it into major and minor selling points. Focus on the strongest, most provocative possibility for a selling idea.

3. *Make your commercial relevant.* It must relate to viewer wants and needs. Make it meaningful to viewers in their own terms. Along with your native imagination and creativity, use taste and discretion. Respect your viewers' sensitivity and intelligence.

4. *Get attention fast—and keep it.* The opening seconds of a spot are vital. These either grab and hold viewer attention or turn if off. But don't just surprise or shock. As soon as possible, let the viewer know what's in it for him or her. Remember, although your ad gains by going after attention, it must hold on to it in order to convince and sell.

5. *Match medium and message.* The format, structure, and style of your commercial should be compatible with each other and with the

product. Also, be sure to match video and audio. They must relate to each other throughout the spot, or you will confuse the viewer.

6. *Stay on track.* While you are developing the elements of your commercial, check back frequently with your strategy statement and marketing objectives.

7. *Don't waste words.* Television is primarily a visual medium, so your video directions should carry more than half the weight of your message. Which comes first, words or pictures? That depends on your own creativity. Try it both ways. Try to visualize as you write, and vice versa. Video instructions should be specific and exact. You will only get what you ask for.

8. *Keep your commercial simple.* Do not cram your spot with too many scenes or too much movement. How much is too much? That depends on the type of spot you are creating. A spot using the spokesperson format needs few scenes. A narrative may require many. On the other hand, avoid long, static scenes. Provide for some movement of camera and/or actors.

9. *Be prepared to revise.* Do not expect to write a final script on the first try. True professionals rewrite and polish material again and again. At some point during the job of writing or sketching your storyboard, you may think of other ways to do the commercial. One of them may be an improvement. If it is, start all over again with it.

Once you are satisfied with your script or storyboard, set it aside. Become a devil's advocate. Look at the script later as objectively as you can. Examine it for impact, clarity, rhythm, pace, persuasion, relevance, and believability. If you do not score well on all of these points, revise.

10. *Write clearly and conversationally.* Write your copy in a natural manner. Avoid the pretentious and the glib. Remember, you are trying to talk to one person whom you do not really know. To paraphrase Shakespeare, "Suit the word to the action"—the mood of the commercial and the personality of the product.

11. *Identify your product.* One of the main reasons why the majority of TV commercials are ineffective is that the brand name has not been implanted strongly. People often recall a bit of action and sometimes remember the product category. But unless you have made a special point of saying—and repeating—the name, it will not stay in your viewer's mind and therefore will not motivate him or her to buy the product.

12. *Time your commercial.* Read it aloud. Act it out. Don't rush it. A pace too fast for the announcer or actor will deprive your spot of its dramatic appeal. And a pace too fast for the viewer will leave him or her far behind.

TV commercials come in varying lengths: 10, 15, 20, 30, and 45 seconds and one or two minutes. On the average, shorter commercials register as well as and sometimes better than longer ones. From a creative point of view, the length of the spot is relatively unimportant. Certainly, you can get more frills into a 30-second commercial than you can into a 10-second one. But it has been proven over and over again that you can deliver a powerful message in a short commercial as effectively as you can in a long one. Of course, the key ingredient, the selling idea, must be presented in a memorable, emphatic way, no matter how long or short the commercial is.

13. *Treat news as news.* If your product is new or has a new feature, give your commercial an announcement flavor. Like newspaper readers, TV viewers appreciate and show interest in something new.

14. *Repeat yourself.* Purposeful repetition can help register a selling idea. Do not expect the viewer to remember something if you say or show it only once in a 30-second spot.

15. *Concentrate on writing, not drawing.* A beautifully drawn storyboard is no substitute for a good selling idea. Storyboards are adequate if they are drawn with stick figures—as long as the idea, along with structure and continuity, comes through.

16. *Give some free rein to the producer.* The storyboard is merely a blueprint. It is prepared so that you and others can better visualize the commercial. The producer should not be completely locked in to every shot shown in the storyboard. Everyone, from the writer to the producer, should have the constant assignment

of trying to make the commercial better, even after final approval.

The TV Storyboard

A commercial producer relies on a script and a storyboard in the same way that a building contractor relies on an architect's specifications and blueprints. Radio commercials require scripts that provide copy and describe sound effects, music, and stage directions. Because it is visual as well as auditory, television needs not only a script, but also an artist's rendering of each scene. This rendering is called a storyboard.

As the TV commercial examples in Chapter 9 show, each frame in the storyboard presents a continuation of some action, a completely new scene, or an addition, such as a superimposed title. The storyboards in Chapter 9 might better be termed "photoboards" insofar as they were taken from finished films. Actual storyboards are rendered in varying degrees of "finish" (See Exhibits 8–1 and 8–2). They are drawn in pencil, felt pen, drawing pen, marker, or wash, or created on a computer. Sometimes photographs are used. When storyboards are completed, they show supervisors, clients, and commercial producers everything they need to know about what will be heard and seen, including locations, sets, actors, special effects, and titles.

A TV storyboard may consist of only one frame to show what will happen in a 10-second spot. Or it may consist of dozens of frames to show what will happen in a two-minute direct response commercial. Video and audio instructions are placed under each frame.

A clear and understandable storyboard is crucial. An easy-to-follow board will aid the evaluators in their approval or disapproval. A good idea with a good structure will show through even a poorly drawn board; conversely, a well-drawn board might also reveal the weakness of a bad idea or a confusing structure.

Storyboard Development

Storyboards can be developed by one person or by a team of writer and artist or writer, artist, and producer. In a team effort, the writer can suggest visual treatments, and the artist can suggest copy changes. At its best, such teamwork stimulates free-wheeling creativity.

For the purpose of this book, assume that you are both writer and art director. It is not important that you be artistically skillful. If you lack drawing talent, use stick figures. With even rudimentary skills, you can indicate the scene, the number and types of people involved in each scene, and the proposed camera angles and distances, from close-up to long shot. However roughly you draw the frames, your storyboard will permit you—and others—to "see" the sequential flow of your commercial, to judge its structure, cohesiveness, and continuity.

In large agencies, a rough (basic) storyboard developed by a writer/artist will be reviewed by a producer (who advises on sets, techniques of camera work, optical effects, and so on), creative supervisors, and account executives. The board may then be sent, with corrections and changes, to the agency "bullpen." Here, the board will be drawn skillfully by sketch artists in a more comprehensive and finished form.

Many people are involved in either creating or passing judgement on the storyboard. If they are imaginative, their suggestions, embellishments, and improvements will show up in the finished product. When agency approval is won, the client's approval is sought. If granted, the commercial heads for production. The producer, director, and director of photography use the storyboard as a guide, a blueprint, and bring their combined expertise to bear.

Exhibit 8–1. Storyboard: Mighty Mite

Advertiser: Eureka   **Title:** "Mighty Mite"
Agency: Keller-Crescent   **Format:** Product Alone
Product: Mighty Mite vacuum   **Length:** 15 seconds

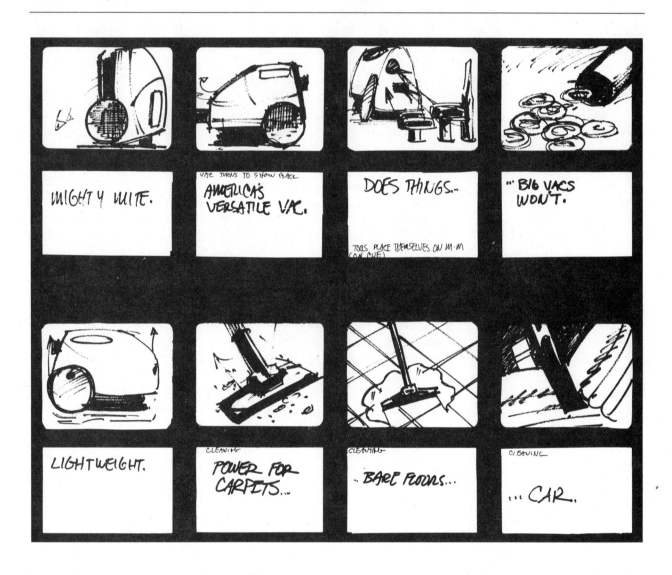

Exhibit 8-2. Storyboard: Oldsmobile Aurora

Advertiser: Oldsmobile

Agency: Leo Burnett

Product: Oldsmobile Aurora

Title: "Aurora: An American Dream"

Format: Fantasy/Special Effects

Length: 30 seconds

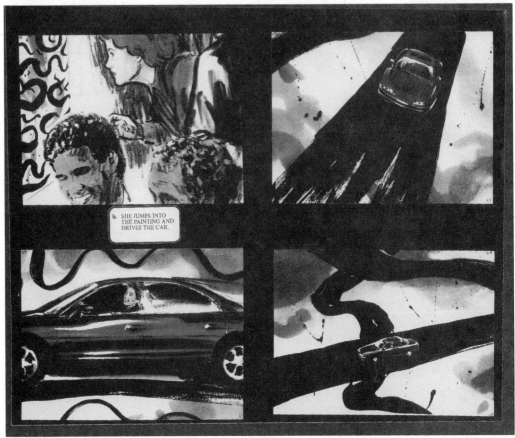

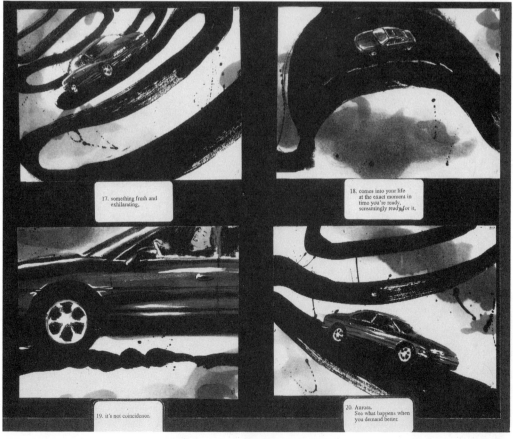

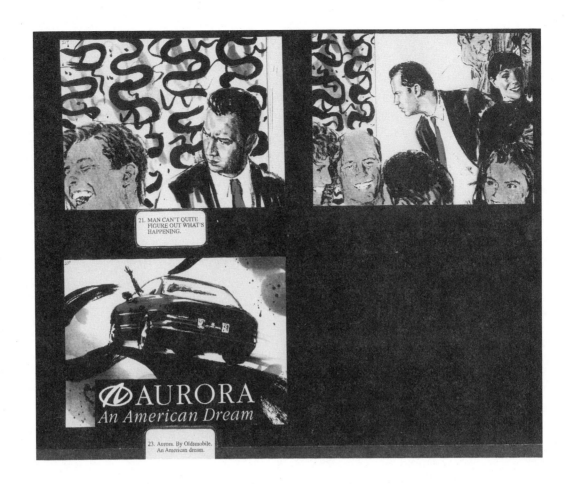

21. MAN CAN'T QUITE FIGURE OUT WHAT'S HAPPENING.

23. Aurora. By Oldsmobile. An American dream.

9

Examples of Successful Television Commercials

The TV commercials in this chapter, like the radio spots in Chapter 6, have been chosen for their excellence—their success in building product awareness, increasing dollar or unit sales, maintaining corporate image, and/or establishing a desirable market position. All were broadcast either nationally or regionally.

Each format discussed in Chapter 3 is represented by one example. In addition, commercials illustrating the use of particular structures (vignettes, continuing series), styles (fantasy, surrealism), and techniques (animation, computer graphics) are included.

The appeal of these commercials rests on their combination of strong selling idea, compatible format, and effective supplementary material. Analyze the strengths (and weaknesses, if any) of each spot, and try to determine the reasons for its success. Think of alternative ways of presenting the sales message. Would a different format work as well? Is the style appropriate? What technique would you have used? What elements would you add to or delete from the commercial?

For each example, we have given the names of the advertiser, the agency, and the product; the title of the spot; the type of format; and the length.

Exhibit 9–1. TV: Hertz ad campaign (first installment)

Advertiser: Hertz

Agency: Wells/Rich/Greene BDDP

Product: Car rental

Title: "Exactly/Family"

Format: Burlesque/Slice-of-Life

Length: 30 seconds

WIFE: Did you reserve the car with Hertz?
HUSBAND: Not exactly, but it's a good deal.

WIFE: Are they as fast as Hertz?
HUSBAND: Not exactly, but what's the rush?

We're on vacation!
ALL KIDS: Yeah!

KID: Dad, are we lost?

WIFE: Hertz gives you computerized directions.

HUSBAND: Honey, this is not exactly Hertz, OK?

WIFE: I hope they have the same

emergency road service

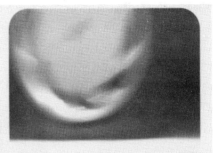

as Hertz.

HUSBAND: Not exactly.
HERTZ PERSON: In rent a car, there's Hertz,

and there's not exactly. Make sure you choose the right one.

WIFE: Are you sure this is the way to the hotel?
HUSBAND: Not exactly. **SFX: HOWL**
WIFE: Did you hear that?

Exhibit 9–2. TV: Hertz ad campaign (second installment)

Advertiser: Hertz

Agency: Wells/Rich/Greene BDDP

Product: Car rental

Title: "Exactly/Boss/REV #1"

Format: Burlesque/Slice-of-Life

Length: 30 seconds

(SFX: AIRPORT NOISES)

BOSS: We've got to move fast, Kirby. I hope you booked Hertz.

KIRBY: Not exactly.

But this company's fast

BOSS: As fast as Hertz #1 Club Gold?
KIRBY: Not exactly. But they

do have special place to pick up the car.

BOSS: Like Hertz?
KIRBY: Not exactly. But it'll be waiting.

BOSS: Under a canopy?

With the keys in it?
KIRBY: Not exactly.

BOSS: …And protected from the weather?

KIRBY: Not exactly.

HERTZ PERSON VO: In rent a car,

HERTZ PERSON: there's Hertz, and there's "Not Exactly." Make sure you choose the right one.

BOSS: Counting on that promotion,

Kirby?
KIRBY: Not exactly.

Exhibit 9–3. Hertz ad campaign (third installment)

Advertiser: Hertz

Agency: Wells/Rich/Greene BDDP

Product: Car rental

Title: "Johnson"

Format: Burlesque/Slice-of-Life

Length: 30 seconds

(MUSIC UP AND UNDER)

MAN 1: Is that Johnson's team behind us?
MAN 2: Exactly.

MAN 3: Are they members of Hertz #1

Gold Club?

MAN 2: Exactly.

MAN 3: Are we members of Hertz #1...
MAN 1: Not... not exactly!

MAN 2: So thanks to Hertz, they're going to get to the meeting on time.

MAN 3: and we'll be late.

MAN 1: So exactly what'll I tell the boss... Hmm?

SPOKESMAN: In rent-a-car, there's Hertz and there's not exactly. Make sure you choose the right one.

MAN 1: And then a dog in the cargo hold ate our presentation.
(MAN 3 BARKS)

MAN 2: Is he buying it?
MAN 1: Not exactly.

Exhibit 9–4. TV: Children's Tylenol

Advertiser: McNeil Consumer Prod. Co.
Agency: Saatchi & Saatchi Compton
Product: Children's Tylenol

Title: "Middle of the Night"
Format: Slice-of-Life
Length: 30 seconds

COMM'L NO.: JJCP 0643

LENGTH: 30 SECONDS

GIRL: Mommy, I feel hot.

MOM: Oh, she's got a fever.

Honey, get the Children's Tylenol.

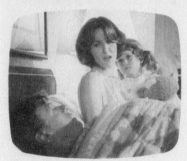

DAD: When did you start using that?

MOM: Ever since I found out Children's Tylenol is the one more pediatricians give their own kids.

ANNCR: (VO) To bring down your child's fever fast,

trust Children's Tylenol.

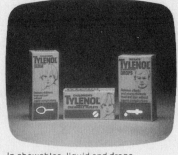

In chewables, liquid and drops.

DAD: Fever's down...

MOM: Pediatricians know what works.
DAD: So do smart mothers.

ANNCR: (VO) To bring down fever fast
trust Children's Tylenol.

It's the one more pediatricians give their
own children.

Exhibit 9–5. TV: Prudential

Advertiser: The Prudential

Agency: Lowe & Partners/SMS

Product: Life Insurance

Title: "Facts of Life"

Format: Slice-of-Life/Narrative

Length: 60 seconds

(SFX: BIRDS)
BOY: Dad?
DAD: Yeah?

BOY: Where do babies come from?
(SFX: WATER)
DAD: Ha, well son, it's like this.

Under specific ovulatory circumstances, a male, female interface may generate an ...

... incipient life form. And over a 9 month time frame, displays incremental growth prior to an ...

... eventual ...
MALE ANNCR: There are some things in this world, you just can't ...

... explain with a lot of fancy talk. DAD: ... determine certain outward characteristics ...

ANNCR: At The Prudential, we believe your life insurance policy is one of them.

(SFX: BKG CONVERSATION) That's why our agents want to be sure you've got it, before you get it.

AGENT: So you understand the advantages of an annuity?

MAN: Ah, sure.
(OLDER WOMAN CLEARS THROAT)

AGENT: Maybe I should just run over that bit again.

ANNCR: Your piece of the rock. We won't let you get it, until you've got it.

Exhibit 9–6. TV: X-14 Mildew Stain Remover

Advertiser: Block Dry Company

Agency: Publicis/Bloom

Product: X-14 Mildew Stain Remover

Title: "Challenge/Judith/Rev. 2"

Format: Testifier/Comparison

Length: 15 seconds

"CHALLENGE/JUDITH/ REV. 2" :15

BDMR 5015

ANNCR VO: We're challenging shoppers

to compare X-14 Mildew Stain Remover

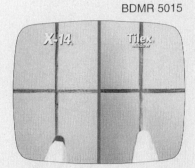

to Tilex.
WOMAN: Oh, look at that.

X-14!

It changed from almost like black

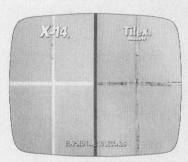

to white. Amazing.

Very amazing.

X-14 is something I would definitely buy.

Exhibit 9–7. TV: Goodyear (1)

Advertiser: Goodyear

Agency: J. Walter Thompson

Product: Aquatred tires

Title: "Skiing"

Format: Demonstration

Length: 30 seconds

AQUATRED

GTBM-9953

(MUSIC THROUGHOUT)
ANNCR: (VO) This is hydroplaning

in less than an inch of water.

And they're not being pulled by a boat,

but by Goodyear Aquatred radials.

Aquatred's deep-groove design channels water away

to keep more tire in contact with the road

for outstanding wet traction.

This is hydroplaning.

This is Aquatreding.

The all season Aquatred only from Goodyear.

It comes with a 60,000 mile treadlife warranty.

Goodyear Aquatred.

Try a set. We like to say:

The best tires in the world

have Goodyear written all over them.

Exhibit 9–8. TV: Goodyear (2)

Advertiser: Goodyear	**Title:** "Tires of the Future"
Agency: J. Walter Thompson	**Format:** Morphing/Demonstration
Product: Goodyear tires	**Length:** 30 seconds

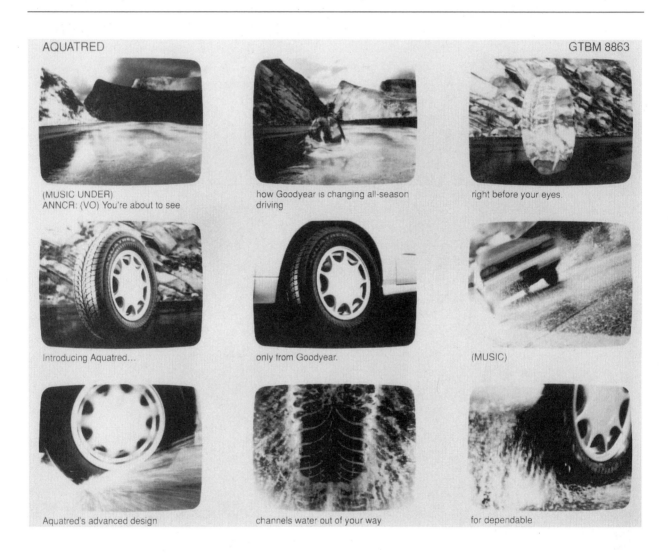

AQUATRED

GTBM 8863

(MUSIC UNDER)
ANNCR: (VO) You're about to see

how Goodyear is changing all-season driving

right before your eyes.

Introducing Aquatred...

only from Goodyear.

(MUSIC)

Aquatred's advanced design

channels water out of your way

for dependable

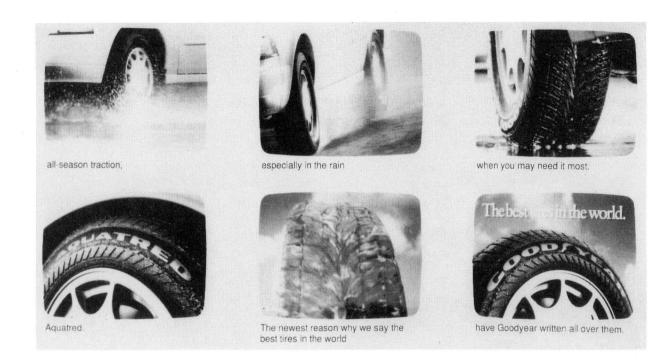

all-season traction,

especially in the rain

when you may need it most.

Aquatred.

The newest reason why we say the best tires in the world

have Goodyear written all over them.

Exhibit 9–9. TV: Zostrix Pain Reliever

Advertiser: Genderm Corporation	**Title:** "Hands"
Agency: Donahoe & Purohit	**Format:** Computer animation
Product: Zostrix Pain Reliever	**Length:** 30 seconds

CLIENT: GENDERM HEALTH CARE

COMM'L NO.: GDZX 5083

ANNCR VO: Are you getting
all the relief you need

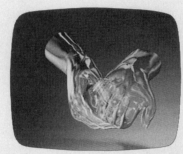

for arthritis pain?

Discover the first in a unique class
of pain reliever doctors have
trusted for years...

Use only as directed for minor arthritis pain.

Zostrix. So effective,

that even though prescriptions
have never been required,

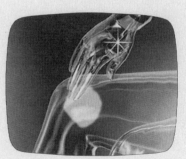

doctors prescribe Zostrix and
triple-strength Zostrix-HP

more than all other topical arthritis
pain relievers combined.

Zostrix is also proven to work hand-
in-hand with oral medications for
added relief, greater mobility.

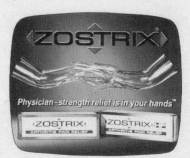

Zostrix: Physician-strength relief
is in your hands.

Exhibit 9–10. TV: Heinz

Advertiser: H. J. Heinz Co.

Agency: Doyle Dane Bernbach, Inc.

Product: Heinz ketchup

Title: "Ketchup Race"

Format: Product alone/Comparison

Length: 30 seconds

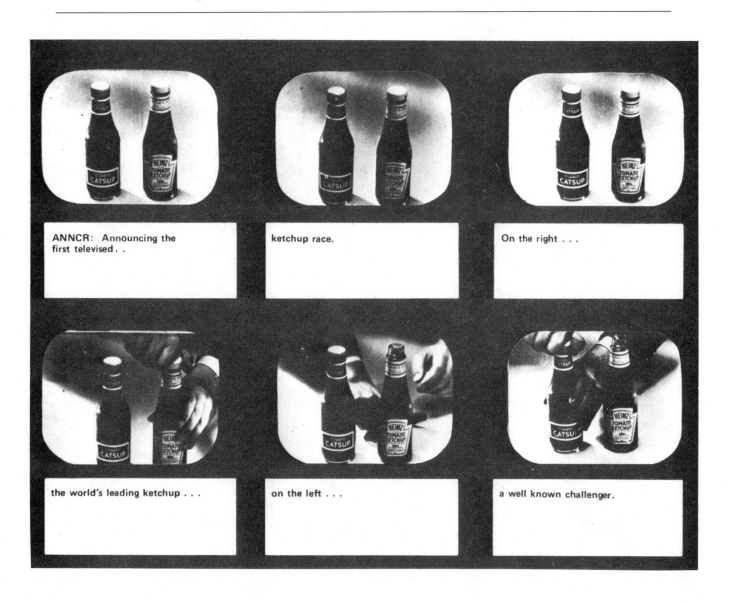

ANNCR: Announcing the first televised..

ketchup race.

On the right . . .

the world's leading ketchup . . .

on the left . . .

a well known challenger.

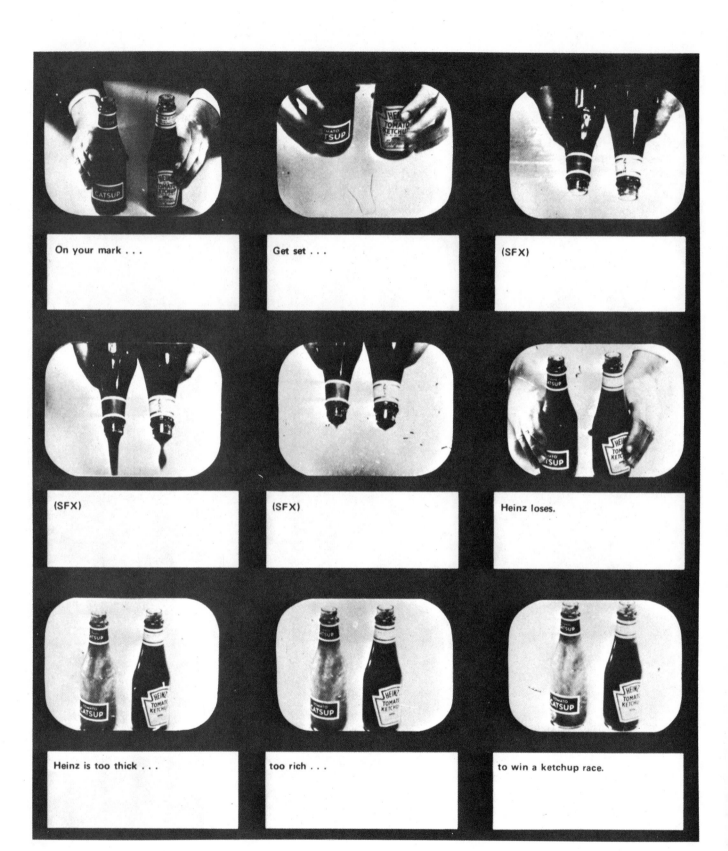

On your mark . . .

Get set . . .

(SFX)

(SFX)

(SFX)

Heinz loses.

Heinz is too thick . . .

too rich . . .

to win a ketchup race.

Exhibit 9–11. TV: Enfamil

Advertiser: Bristol-Myers Squibb Co.
Agency: J. Walter Thompson
Product: Enfamil Toddler Formula

Title: "Baby Drops Bottle"
Format: Narrative
Length: 30 seconds

(MUSIC) WOMAN: She's at that certain age. (SFX: BABY SOUND IN & OUT) She's not an infant anymore,

she's not quite a young lady, (SFX: BABY SOUND IN & OUT)

she's a toddler. Too big for a bottle, (SFX: BABY SOUND IN & OUT) not big enough for a glass.

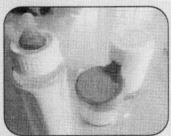

Ah this is just right,

new Next Step Toddler Formula, from the makers of Enfamil.

(SFX: BABY SOUND IN & OUT)

Especially designed for toddlers,

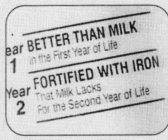

with the iron cow's milk lacks.

WOMAN: Here sweetheart. (SFX: BABY SOUND IN & OUT)

WOMAN: After the bottle, before the milk. New Next Step Toddler Formula.

In Soy too.

(SFX: BABY SOUND IN & OUT) (MUSIC OUT)

Exhibit 9–12. TV: Norwegian Cruise Line

Advertiser: Norwegian-American
Agency: Goodby, Silverstein & Partners
Product: Cruises

Title: "Constitution/Underwater"
Format: Fantasy
Length: 30 seconds

VIDEO:

Open on a tracking shot across white sand with sea and sky beyond.
SUPER: A NEW CONSTITUTION FOR THE WORLD

Cut to CU of a woman.

Cut to a man and the woman both in white on white sand dappled with light from above. Suddenly the two become one in a spontaneous embrace.
SUPER: ARTICLE 1, WE SHALL FORM A MORE PERFECT UNION.

Cut to CU of the woman. The man kisses her neck as she reaches around, talking to the camera.

Dissolve back to a beautiful underwater shot tracking past a wipe of coral to reveal two persons in an embrace amongst the coral and flora and fish.
SUPER: ARTICLE 3, WINTER WILL BE EXILED.

Cut to ECU of the woman as she speaks to the camera.
Cut to the woman walking alone on a sandbar.

Cut to a shot of the ship with waves.
SUPER: IT'S DIFFERENT OUT HERE.
NORWEGIAN CRUISE LINE.
SHIPS REGISTRY BAHAMAS.

AUDIO:

WOMAN VO: **A new constitution for the World.**

SFX: COWBOY JUNKIES "BLUE MOON" IN BACKGROUND.
Article 1, Section 3.

Article 3.

Winter will be exiled.

Article 6, Section 6.

Article 10, Section 1. There will be peace and hope

and really good food.

**It's Different Out Here.
Norwegian Cruise Line.**

Exhibit 9–13. TV: *Sports Illustrated*

Advertiser: Time-Warner

Agency: Wunderman Cato Johnson

Product: *Sports Illustrated*

Title: "Video Store"

Format: Burlesque/Slice-of-Life

Length: 120 seconds

1. (MUSIC UNDER)
(SFX: SOUNDS OF CAR)
MAN: Hi! I've been looking all over for this terrific video cassette I heard about...

2. it's called "Not So Great Moments In Sports."

3. Like one scene is where Billy Martin tries to give an ump a shoe shine.

4. SALESMAN: That's a fantastic video. My favorite part is where John McEnroe plays tennis with his orange juice.

5. MAN: I hear there's a scene where Reggie Jackson protests a Gaylord Perry spitball with a visual aid.

6. SALESMAN: I love it where a kicker tries to play quarterback.

7. "Not So Great Moments" is forty-five minutes of the funniest sports footage I've ever seen.

8. MAN: Great! So you have it? SALESMAN: No. It's not in video stores yet.

9. MAN: Now, what do I do? SALESMAN: You get it free.

10. MAN: Lemme understand... you don't have the video, but you're gonna tell me how to get it free. SALESMAN: Right.

11. MAN: Am I missing something?

12. SALESMAN: You're missing out on Sports Illustrated. MAN: Sports Illustrated! I love S.I.

13. What does Sports Illustrated have to do with it?

14. SALESMAN: You get "Not So Great Moments In Sports," free with your paid subscription.

15. MAN: Ooh...I let my subscription run out.

1. SALESMAN: Well, now's the perfect time to go for it again.

2. You get twenty-five weeks of America's best sports coverage, including the Pro Football Spectacular with all the picks, previews and profiles,

3. and the beautiful Swimsuit Issue. MAN: I like that. SALESMAN: (VO) Everybody likes that.

4. You even get a handy NFL Schedule.

5. MAN: And "Not So Great Moments In Sports"?

6. SALESMAN: You get it all. MAN: I do? How?

7. SALESMAN: Just call Sports Illustrated's toll free number. MAN: Wait a minute! All that great footage has gotta be worth a fortune.

8. SALESMAN: I oughta know... MAN: Yeah, I bet they raised the price of the magazine, right? Uh-uh, it's over 47% off the cover price.

9. Just three installments of $9.89 each. You can even put it on a credit card.

10. MAN: (VO) No kiddin'? I get twenty-five weeks of S.I., including the Pro Football Spectacular, the Football Schedule...

11. the Swimsuit Issue...and video cassette - free? SALESMAN: You get it all. Just call 1-800-321-8900.

12. MAN: I've gotta get to a phone. What's the number again?

13. SALESMAN: Here... 1-800-321-8900.

14. MAN 2: Whew!...Hi, have you heard of "Not So Great Moments In Sports"?

15. SALESMAN AND MAN 1: (LAUGH)

Exhibit 9-14. TV: Star-Kist

Advertiser: Star-Kist Foods, Inc.

Agency: Leo Burnett Co.

Product: Star-Kist tuna

Title: "Ten More"

Format: Slice-of-life/Animation

Length: 30 seconds

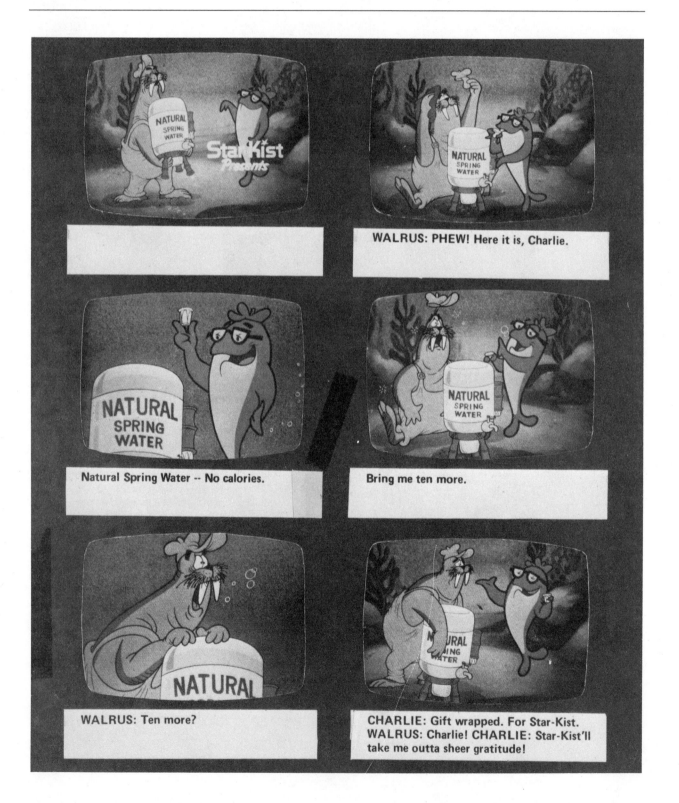

WALRUS: PHEW! Here it is, Charlie.

Natural Spring Water -- No calories.

Bring me ten more.

WALRUS: Ten more?

CHARLIE: Gift wrapped. For Star-Kist.
WALRUS: Charlie! CHARLIE: Star-Kist'll take me outta sheer gratitude!

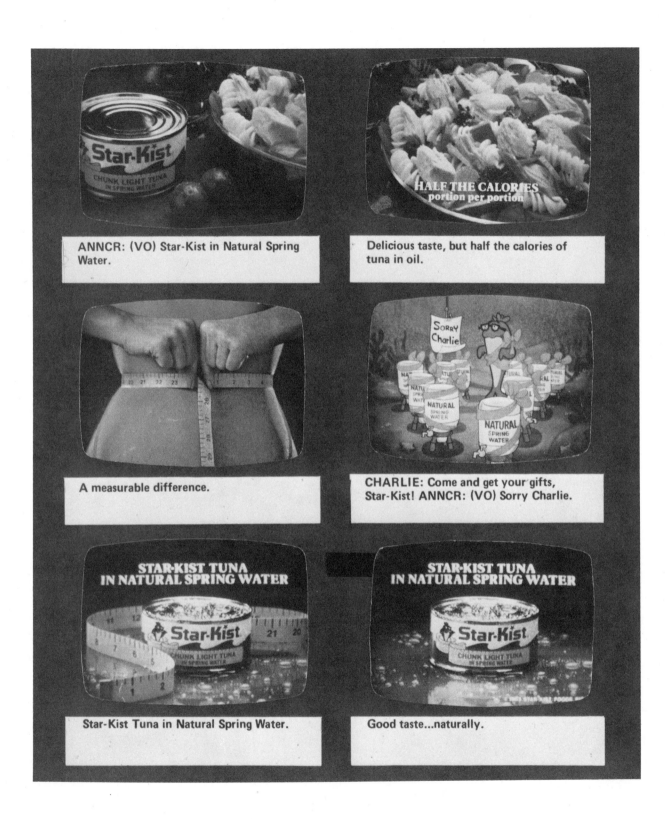

ANNCR: (VO) Star-Kist in Natural Spring Water.

Delicious taste, but half the calories of tuna in oil.

A measurable difference.

CHARLIE: Come and get your gifts, Star-Kist! ANNCR: (VO) Sorry Charlie.

Star-Kist Tuna in Natural Spring Water.

Good taste...naturally.

10

Television Assignments

The assignments in this chapter, like those in Chapter 7, allow you to try your hand at writing commercials. Before you start, turn back to Chapters 2, 3, and 4 to review the fundamentals of writing and advertising elements. Remember, in writing television commercials, you have more techniques to work with and more elements to handle. For this reason, you must choose your components very carefully, paying special attention to unity and coherence. Avoid the temptation to include too much: After all, it's difficult to get everything working together smoothly and effectively.

For help in generating good ideas, review the guidelines in Chapter 8, and look over the TV commercials in Chapter 9. Do not be afraid to use a variation on someone else's successful idea.

Again, you are given background data, a set of marketing/advertising objectives, or a print, TV, or radio ad. Examine this material thoroughly, and use it as a foundation for writing your strategy statement. Periodically check your developing commercial against the product facts, your objectives, and the selling theme contained in your strategy.

For each assignment, use the script sheet or storyboard form provided and follow the style shown in Chapter 9: if you need additional script sheets or storyboard forms, photocopy a blank one. Indicate advertiser, format, product, and length. Double-space all assignments. Type names of speakers, sound effects, video directions, and music cues and copy in caps. Type nonmusical copy in upper and lower case letters. For TV scripts, follow the style shown in Exhibit 10–1.

Exhibit 10-1. TV Script: Coors Light

Advertiser: Adolph Coors Co. **Title:** "Camping"
Agency: Foote, Cone & Belding **Format:** Musical
Product: Coors Light beer **Length:** 60 seconds

VIDEO

AUDIO

OPEN ON BACK OF CAB, WEIGHED DOWN ON ONE SIDE.

(MUSIC UNDER)

JIM(VO): After the loads I carry all day, it's time to pick up speed.

CUT TO JIM, THE CAB DRIVER, IN A SERIES OF THREE PASSENGER SHOTS: HEAVY-SET WOMAN: BUSINESSMEN PILED INTO BACK SEAT, HOLDING A MEETING: A CAMERA-HAPPY TOURIST COUPLE.

CUT TO CAB DRIVING OUT OF FRAME.

CUT TO "TURN IT LOOSE" NEON GRAPHIC.

SINGERS: TURN IT LOOSE,
TURN IT LOOSE,
TURN IT LOOSE TONIGHT.

VAN DRIVES INTO FRAME AND STOPS.

CUT TO JIM WITH COOLER. HE HITS VAN DOORS, HINGED SPEAKERS FALL DOWN.

CUT TO JIM TOSSING BEER TO HIS GIRL, SHERRY.

COORS LIGHT, COORS LIGHT

CUT TO UNENDING TRAIN OF FRIENDS CLIMBING OUT OF VAN, INCLUDING MOOSE, THE CHIPS-AND-BEER BUDDY.

TURN IT LOOSE TONIGHT.

CUT TO JIM LIGHTING FIRE, AS SHERRY WATCHES. HIS LIGHTER WON'T WORK, SO HE USES A BLOW TORCH.

DON'T HOLD BACK,

CUT TO TENT ALMOST UP.

DON'T HOLD BACK,

CUT TO JIM TURNING UP STEREO VOLUME.

TURN IT

CUT TO FRIEND, SAM, CONTENT TO SPEND THE EVENING IN THE VAN, TURNING UP VOLUME.	LOOSE TONIGHT.
CUT TO ELDERLY COUPLE, SURPRISED AT THE NOISE.	(COORS LIGHT)
CUT TO SHOT OF SHERRY SITTING ON COOLER. PEOPLE TAKE BEERS FROM COOLER, AS SHE SCOOTS UP AND DOWN (ALA CHOW-CHOW-CHOW).	BEER AFTER BEER WHEN YOU'RE MOVING AROUND
CU COORS LIGHT CAN WITH SWEAT DRIPPING.	COORS LIGHT
CUT TO JIM AND FRIENDS, WITH SURPRISED LOOKS.	IS THE ONE.
CUT TO THE TENT, COLLAPSING, WITH A FIGURE OF SOMEONE UNDERNEATH. A FLASHLIGHT TURNS ON.	THAT WON'T SLOW YOU DOWN.
CUT TO CU COORS LIGHT CAN BEING HELD.	COORS LIGHT
CUT TO MOOSE EMERGING FROM TENT, WITH CHIPS AND BEER INTACT.	TURN IT LOOSE TONIGHT.
CUT TO JIM, SEATED ON TINY CAMPING STOOL. HE LAUGHS SO HARD, HE FALLS OVER BACKWARD.	TURN IT LOOSE
CUT TO ELDERLY COUPLE, WITH BEERS, LAUGHING.	(LAUGHTER)
CUT TO CU COORS LIGHT CAN BEING OPENED.	SINGERS: TURN IT LOOSE! 　　　　　(COORS LIGHT!)
SUPER: *TURN IT LOOSE!*	

Assignment 10-1: Background Data

THE CLIENT: Campbell Soup Co.

THE PRODUCT: V-8 Cocktail vegetable juice is a canned red juice consisting of eight natural vegetable juices: tomato, carrot, celery, parsley, beets, spinach, watercress, and lettuce. The blend is approximately 70 percent tomato juice and 30 percent other juices.

THE MARKET: According to a survey report, one out of five people sampled used V-8 on a regular basis. The product is used as a breakfast drink; for lunch, dinner, and snacks; as a cocktail ingredient; and in soups. V-8 is currently positioned in the red juice/vegetable juice market, which is about three-fourths tomato juice and one-fourth vegetable juice. The principal users and nonusers of V-8 are as follows. A disproportionate amount of vegetable juice is consumed by the 50 plus age group. These users account for 57 percent of consumption. Use of V-8 is very low among the younger age groups, especially the 18 to 24-year-old segment. It appears that there is a great potential for sales of the product to college students.

THE PACKAGE: V-8 comes in various can sizes, including 46-ounces, 6-packs, and mini 6-packs.

DISTRIBUTION: V-8 is distributed primarily in retail grocery and food stores. Some 12-ounce cans are available in vending machines.

PRICE: The product is priced slightly higher than tomato juice.

AD BUDGET: $3,750,000.

MARKETING PROBLEM: To get people 18–35 to drink more V-8 more often.

1. Write a script for a 30-second slice-of-life commercial.

2. Write a 30-second comparison commercial in any format.

Television Script Sheet

Student name: **Advertiser:**
Date submitted: **Product:**
Commercial length: **Format:**

VIDEO   AUDIO

Television Script Sheet
_____

Student name: **Advertiser:**
Date submitted: **Product:**
Commercial length: **Format:**
_____

                    VIDEO   AUDIO

Assignment 10–2: Background Data

THE CLIENT: Farmer's Friend, Inc.

THE PRODUCT: Viravac is an insoluble herbicide that is mixed into the top two or three inches of soil, where 90 percent of the weed seeds germinate. The farmer may use his or her own disc or field cultivator to apply the herbicide. Viravac does not need rain to make it work. It stays put because it attaches itself to the surface of soil particles and organic matter. This is a great advantage over other herbicides, which are less absorptive. Other advantages: Viravac goes to work immediately to kill susceptible germinating grass, and it keeps working even in heavy rain. It gives long-lasting weed control all summer long, the result of which is a cleaner field with a faster, earlier harvest.

THE MARKET: Viravac is used primarily by soybean, cotton, and sunflower farmers, especially in dry climates.

THE PACKAGE: The product is sold in 80-pound bags. "Viravac" is printed in three-inch letters across the top of the front, and directions for application are given in small print on the bottom two-thirds. Chemical contents are printed on the back.

DISTRIBUTION: Viravac is sold in the South and Midwest at farm supply stores.

PRICE: Although Viravac is slightly more expensive than other herbicides, it requires less product per acre.

AD BUDGET: $100,000 annually

MARKETING PROBLEM: Nonusers of Viravac think it is too expensive and therefore use competitive products.

1. Write a script for a 30-second demonstration commercial for regional broadcast.

2. Write a 30-second testimonial.

Television Script Sheet

Student name: **Advertiser:**

Date submitted: **Product:**

Commercial length: **Format:**

VIDEO   AUDIO

Television Script Sheet

Student name: **Advertiser:**
Date submitted: **Product:**
Commercial length: **Format:**

VIDEO   AUDIO

Assignment 10–3: Background Data

THE CLIENT: Carson Cosmetics, Inc.

THE PRODUCT: Silk 'n Soft is a revolutionary therapeutic hand lotion that actually works with the chemistry of the skin to soften, protect, and heal, as no other lotion can. It moisturizes the top layers of the skin at once and stays on the skin longer, even when exposed to water. The white, creamy lotion has a light, herbal fragrance.

THE MARKET: Potential buyers are women aged 24 and up, mainly homemakers.

THE PACKAGE: The product is sold in a 16-ounce, gray plastic squeeze bottle with a matching dispenser top. A four-color photo of a woman's hands is set in the middle of the front of the bottle. The burgundy words "SILK 'N SOFT" are printed in a semicircle over the hands.

DISTRIBUTION: Silk 'n Soft will be sold in national chain and independent drug stores and in the health and beauty departments of discount and grocery stores.

PRICE: $4.25 per bottle, about 50 cents higher than other therapeutic lotions.

AD BUDGET: $1 million for national rollout.

MARKETING PROBLEM: Other cosmetics with better-known brand names have captured the lion's share of the therapeutic hand lotion market.

1. Prepare a storyboard for a 30-second problem-solution commercial.

2. Prepare a 30-second spokesperson commercial with music.

TV Storyboard Form

_____

Student name: **Advertiser:**
Date submitted: **Product:**
Commercial length: **Format:**

_____

VIDEO

AUDIO

VIDEO

AUDIO

VIDEO

AUDIO

Television Script Sheet

Student name: **Advertiser:**

Date submitted: **Product:**

Commercial length: **Format:**

VIDEO   AUDIO

THE CLIENT: Chase-Pitkin

THE PRODUCT: Chase-Pitkin, a well-established and respected hardware store, is running a special Memorial Day promotion. The sale features name-brand gas barbecues ranging in price from under $200 to almost $400.

THE MARKET: The promotion is aimed at outdoor barbecue enthusiasts in up-state New York.

THE PACKAGE: Buy a $199.95 barbecue and get a set of cooking utensils. Buy a $299.95 barbecue and get a set of cooking utensils and an extra propane tank. Buy a $399.95 barbecue and get a set of cooking utensils, an extra propane tank, and an electric rotisserie.

DISTRIBUTION: The sale will be held at all Chase-Pitkin outlets.

PRICE: $199.95 to $399.95.

AD BUDGET: $100,000 for this promotion.

MARKETING PROBLEM: To communicate all the offers and run a successful sale on a very modest budget.

1. Prepare a storyboard for a 30-second spot using a spokesperson.

2. Prepare a 30-second commercial in the product-alone format.

TV Storyboard Form

Student name: **Advertiser:**
Date submitted: **Product:**
Commercial length: **Format:**

VIDEO

AUDIO

VIDEO

AUDIO

VIDEO

AUDIO

TV Storyboard Form

Student name: **Advertiser:**

Date submitted: **Product:**

Commercial length: **Format:**

VIDEO

AUDIO

VIDEO

AUDIO

VIDEO

AUDIO

Assignment 10–5: Marketing Objectives

MARKETING: Hitachi is Japan's largest manufacturer of home electronics equipment. However, in the United States, Sony and Panasonic are better known. Hitachi wishes to (1) reach a greater number of potential buyers with prime-time television; (2) encourage dealers and distributors to carry the full line of company products; and (3) increase the public's awareness of the company as a total home electronics manufacturer.

ADVERTISING: The television campaign should (1) show Hitachi as a manufacturer of a full range of home electronics products—including color TV, black and white TV, clock radios, stereo systems, tape recorders, walk-along radios, and VCRs; (2) support and enhance the company's quality image through pride of ownership; and (3) continue to present company products in a human setting.

1. Write a script for a 60-second slice-of-life commercial.

2. Write a 30-second spinoff.

Television Script Sheet

Student name: **Advertiser:**

Date submitted: **Product:**

Commercial length: **Format:**

VIDEO	AUDIO

Television Script Sheet

Student name: **Advertiser:**
Date submitted: **Product:**
Commercial length: **Format:**

VIDEO	AUDIO

Assignment 10–6: Marketing Objectives

MARKETING: Research shows that "prior experience with the brand" and "advice of a friend or relative" are two of the strongest influences on consumer preferences among house paints. Glidden, a major manufacturer of interior and exterior house paint, believes that a candid camera testimonial campaign would exploit these research findings.

ADVERTISING: The advertising agency agrees to use hidden-camera technique in a interview with a real user. The campaign has three objectives: (1) to show customer satisfaction with the quality of Glidden's product by emphasizing particular attributes; (2) to demonstrate the strong brand loyalty among company product users; and (3) to create believability.

1. Prepare a storyboard for a 30-second testimonial spot.

2. Prepare a 15-second spinoff.

TV Storyboard Form

Student name: **Advertiser:**

Date submitted: **Product:**

Commercial length: **Format:**

VIDEO

AUDIO

VIDEO

AUDIO

VIDEO

AUDIO

TV Storyboard Form

Student name: **Advertiser:**
Date submitted: **Product:**
Commercial length: **Format:**

VIDEO

AUDIO

VIDEO

AUDIO

VIDEO

AUDIO

Assignment 10–7: Fact Sheet

The following fact sheet should be used in the writing assignments given below. The advertiser is the Australian Trade Commission.

PRODUCTS: Australian apples and pears

- A fresh supply of Australian apples and pears has just arrived.
- Two varieties of pears are Bosc and Parkhams (Park-ums).
- Both are sweet and succulent and have a distinctive taste.
- They may look like domestic pears, but their taste is superior—their flesh is white and aromatic.
- Pears shipped to the United States are the best of a vintage crop.
- The apples are called "Granny Smith" apples.
- Green in color, they are nevertheless magnificent eating apples.
- These apples can also be used in cooking.
- Now available in grocery stores and supermarkets at a price about the same as domestic apples and pears.
- More and more people are asking for them, so hurry—before they are sold out.

1. Write a script for a 30-second commercial in the product-alone format.

2. Write a 30-second spot in any format.

Television Script Sheet

Student name:	**Advertiser:**
Date submitted:	**Product:**
Commercial length:	**Format:**

VIDEO   AUDIO

Television Script Sheet

Student name: **Advertiser:**

Date submitted: **Product:**

Commercial length: **Format:**

VIDEO   AUDIO

Assignment 10-8: Rewrite

The following radio script begins and ends with an appeal to "looking good." It also emphasizes that savings come from low prices and good service. The two-pronged sales pitch, spiced up with a special offer, is neatly wrapped in a memorable rhyme that serves as the company's slogan. Make up a name for the company and revise the spot for TV according to the directions given below.

1. Write a script for a 60-second revision of this commercial as a TV demonstration.

2. Write a 30-second television spot in any format.

ANNCR:

"Look sharp and you feel sharp." That's an old saying that still goes at (ADVERTISER). They know that a freshly pressed shirt and a spotlessly clean suit can make a real difference in the way you feel—and the way you come across. You can count on (ADVERTISER) for professional laundering and dry cleaning...and at prices that may surprise you. Shirts washed and pressed, only (PRICE) each. Suits or sport coats dry cleaned, just (PRICE); slacks, (PRICE) each. Bulk laundry, sorted, washed and folded, (PRICE). (ADVERTISER) uses the most modern equipment and the safest techniques to take good care of your laundry and dry cleaning. Clothes are a big investment, and having your clothes professionally dry cleaned will help them last longer. So check the closet and the clothes hamper, then stop in at (ADVERTISER), (LOCATION), on the way to work or home tomorrow. Mention (STATION) and you'll also qualify for an additional (percent) off any of our services. (ADVERTISER). Where the best dressed take their cleaning for less.

Television Script Sheet

Student name: **Advertiser:**

Date submitted: **Product:**

Commercial length: **Format:**

VIDEO   AUDIO

Television Script Sheet

Student name: **Advertiser:**

Date submitted: **Product:**

Commercial length: **Format:**

VIDEO	AUDIO

Assignment 10–9: Rewrite

Look at the headline, visual, and body copy of the Frigidaire ad below. What do you think the main message is? Write a television commercial based on the same selling idea.

1. Write a script for a 30-second commercial in the vignette format.

2. Write a 30-second commercial in the problem-solution format.

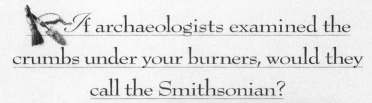

Sealed top,
no crumbs,
no fossils.

CONTOUR CONCEPT
SCULPTED DESIGN THAT
LOOKS AND WORKS BETTER

No archaeological dig site here. The new Frigidaire Gallery™ electric range can actually help keep itself clean. It was developed with Contour Concept™ design based on the way you use it. Flowing lines, softer edges, and fewer grease-collecting seams make it a breeze to clean. And the large convection oven, which features six broiling temperatures, is self-cleaning. The electric range (halogen optional) also has expandable burners for different pan sizes. See the Frigidaire Gallery line of appliances at your retailer, or call 1-800-FRIGIDAIRE for our free brochure. **FRIGIDAIRE**

Frigidaire Gallery · The look of better performance.

Television Script Sheet

Student name: **Advertiser:**

Date submitted: **Product:**

Commercial length: **Format:**

VIDEO   AUDIO

Television Script Sheet

Student name: **Advertiser:**
Date submitted: **Product:**
Commercial length: **Format:**

VIDEO	AUDIO

Examine the headline, visual, and body copy of the Volvo ad below. What do you think the main message is? Write a television commercial based on the same selling idea?

1. Write a script for a 30-second commercial in the narrative format.

2. Write a 30-second comparison.

Television Script Sheet

Student name: **Advertiser:**

Date submitted: **Product:**

Commercial length: **Format:**

VIDEO   AUDIO

Television Script Sheet

___

Student name: **Advertiser:**

Date submitted: **Product:**

Commercial length: **Format:**

___

VIDEO   AUDIO

Assignment 10–11: Rewrite

The following print ad was accompanied by "primitive" drawings of a Perrier bottle cap above and four prehistoric-looking animals below. Study the copy and revise the ad for television as directed.

BORN SALT-FREE.

Prehistoric cuisine was salt-free, of course. If you could manage to make a fire, you were ahead of the game. And if the game was well-done, you were a four-star chef. Because stone-age man didn't know there was such a thing as salt. Or high-blood pressure, either.

And his favorite libation came from a pure, sparkling, naturally salt-free spring. The spring we now call Perrier. Earth's first soft drink.

Today, modern man is over-salted. He salts his peas, his porterhouse, his peanuts. Most of his soft drinks, even the diet drinks, are salted, too.

Not Perrier. Perrier has been salt-free since the day it was born. And while other beverages have had to change their contents, the only thing we've had to change is our label. Just to let you know.

Perrier. Earth's First Soft Drink.™

1. Prepare a storyboard for a 30-second spot in the slice-of-life format using fantasy.

2. Prepare a 30-second commercial in any format.

TV Storyboard Form

Student name: **Advertiser:**
Date submitted: **Product:**
Commercial length: **Format:**

VIDEO

AUDIO

VIDEO

AUDIO

VIDEO

AUDIO

TV Storyboard Form

Student name:

Date submitted:

Commercial length:

Advertiser:

Product:

Format:

VIDEO

AUDIO

VIDEO

AUDIO

VIDEO

AUDIO

Television Script Sheet

Student name: **Advertiser:**
Date submitted: **Product:**
Commercial length: **Format:**

VIDEO   AUDIO

Section Four

Broadcast Considerations

11

Producing the Commercial

The producer will take over after you have finished the research and written a focused, tightly worded script with a strong selling idea, the agency and the client have approved the commercial, and the budget has been okayed.

This isn't to say that the producer will not get involved until this point. Ideally, the creators of the commercial have worked closely with the producer. The producer has assisted and guided you with his or her imagination and technical expertise. From now on, the producer is in charge, and you will assist and guide.

The Producer's Role

Some producers work for production firms; some are strictly free-lance. For our example let's assume the producer is on staff at the agency. What does he or she do?

First, the producer should know the ins and outs of radio, film, tape, and digital media. With that knowledge as a base, the producer works from both a creative and a practical point of view. The creative point of view helps bring about an imaginative and professional selling message. At the same time, the practical point of view means working within the production budget, keeping production moving ahead, and being the hub around which a dozen or more phases of commercial making are like the spokes of a wheel. The producer combines artistic and business sense under one hat, because only a

combination of these polarized talents will result in an effective commercial.

Even though the expense of producing a radio commercial is a fraction of the cost of a TV commercial, the same care, creativity, and professionalism must be devoted to it. The basic principles and concerns that apply to TV production apply to radio, with possibly one major exception: Radio production is rarely given over to "outside" production houses. Therefore, there is no bidding system.

The agency producer normally handles every detail, such as the booking of a studio, the hiring of a qualified sound engineer and a sound effects person, casting, the quality reproduction of the master tape, and so on. Usually, however, when a jingle or original music is required, the agency hires an outside contractor who handles the creation and production of the jingle or music, reporting to the agency producer. Although the rest of this chapter deals specifically with TV production, you should be aware that the same guidelines and virtually the same steps apply to radio production.

Producing for TV

After the commercial is approved, the television producer has several copies of the storyboard made. These are sent for bids to production houses, which have been selected from a long list as best qualified for this particular type of commercial. The number of bids varies. Some agencies and clients insist on as many as five bids. The norm is three. Still others, having had an agreeable experience with a particular firm's work in the past, may opt for that house, if the price is acceptable.

Production houses may generalize or specialize. Animation may be one firm's forte; shooting automobiles may be another's; and sensitivity toward talent may be yet another's. The producer takes this into consideration when the storyboard is sent out for bids. The producer also considers each firm's past performance, directors on staff, current output, adherence to shooting schedules, production talent, and ability to deliver on time. And, of course, the price.

When the selection has been made, a contract is drawn up between the agency (acting in behalf of the client) and the production house. Nothing is left to chance or to memory. A commercial represents a big investment for the client, and production costs continue to go up each year.

Preproduction Meeting

The preproduction conference is a meeting of minds. It is attended by the client and the production house representatives, including producer and director. The agency representatives include writer, art director, and account executive. The meeting is chaired by the agency producer.

At the preproduction meeting, the storyboard is reviewed frame by frame and sequence by sequence. All suggestions and refinements are focused on meeting the commercial's objective. Ideas are exchanged on sets, actors, sound effects, music—every facet of the spot. Agreement and understanding are reached, a shooting schedule is planned, and the production house goes to work. It sets aside studio time for the shooting and arranges for the crew. If locations are indicated in the storyboard, the house agrees with the agency producer on a scouting date.

From this meeting on, the agency producer is in day-to-day contact with the production firm. The details are multitudinous. Sets must be designed, and the sketches must be approved. Props are gathered, ordered, or built. Costumes are agreed on. The director selects a director of photography and a camera operator; art work and titles are executed and approved. Not even the smallest detail should go unplanned.

Auditions are held for actors and announcers. (The casting procedure is examined at length later in this chapter.)

The Shooting Date

Your commercial might be shot on a studio sound stage. Unfortunately, last-minute preparation is the rule rather than the exception. Final touches are given to the set, and the property master arranges the props (including duplicates and triplicates, in case of breakage or soilage).

The agency producer is in authority on the set. He or she works closely with the production house team, constantly consulting with director, camera operator, and crew chiefs. Lighting is set for the first scene. Actors rehearse, get their makeup, rehearse some more. And after much coffee and prune danish, the assistant director calls for quiet on the set, and the director goes for Take One, Scene One.

Because time in the studio is so valuable, the producer and director will work fast. Camera moves will be plotted and written on the script. The actors learn their marks and cues. The technical director (responsible for picture quality), the sound engineer, the camera operators, and the director all work as a team to give the commercial professional smoothness and pace.

As the creator of this commercial, you are in evidence. You observe. You comment, but for everyone's sanity you restrict your comments to one person—the agency producer, the man or woman in charge. He or she will relay your observations and suggestions to the director. You may wonder if a piece of business may be acted differently to get a better effect. You may question an on-camera reading or prefer a tighter close-up of the product than the director has set up. The more you learn about production, the more valuable your suggestions will become, and, consequently, the more experience you will bring to your next creative assignment.

Take follows take, scene follows scene. Often, the pace seems snail-like, but professionalism includes a large dose of patience. Use it. And finally, after a good take on the last scene, the shooting portion of this production is wrapped up.

Sound and Music

Your commercial may require that the sound track be recorded simultaneously with the shooting, especially if actors are involved in a problem-solution structure. Or, if the commercial calls for an announcer voice-over, chances are good that the producer will tape the audio track before the studio date.

At this taping session, held in a sound studio, the announcer and/or actors work with the script, rehearsing it under the direction of the agency producer. Sound experts monitor the voice levels, adjust microphones for position, and keep a log of the takes. The length of the session depends on the complexity of the commercial and the talents of the announcer and actors. At this session, the writer contributes suggestions as to inflections, emphasis, pacing, and so on. He or she is sometimes asked to rewrite a sequence that may be awkward to read. A writer can often improve a commercial in the recording studio, just as at the actual shooting, by constantly being alert to the possibilities of enhancing the commercial's communicability—or, in plain English, by making the persuasion and sell come through.

Music and sound effects may be recorded at this session or at separate sessions. Recording gives a producer flexibility. He or she can record voice, sound effects, or music on separate tracks. If the music has been selected from "stock"—a large bank of music and musical effects that is readily available in large cities—that music is transferred to tape. If musicians and singers are used, this recording session is set up and conducted in a manner similar to the announcer's.

At last, the producer has, say, three tapes: announcer, music, and sound effects. They are transferred to 35mm magnetic tape. The producer then arranges for a mix. At a sound studio with multitrack facilities, the three tapes are placed on separate reels, synchronized for time, and run. The sound engineer "mixes" the tracks together, combines them, each with its own level of volume. The result is a single track with all the sound combined, each at the proper level and intensity.

Completing the Commercial

The producer has many things to do to complete a commercial, and all at just the same time. If you are filming your commercial, the "dailies" will be available on the day following the shooting date. Dailies are the takes that met on-set approval for printing. The dailies will be transferred to videotape or onto a computer system for editing. Of course, if you are shooting a videotape, your dailies are immediately available for viewing and scene selection. The scenes are assembled into a "rough cut"—the first approximation of the actual commercial.

When approvals are given on the rough cut, the original footage (if you shot on film) is transferred to tape. Then the commercial is conformed to the rough cut in an on-line editing suite. Special effects and titles are added. Cuts or dissolves are incorporated. If the sound track was not included before, it is now.

The producer's job is almost over. And so is yours, as creator, at least for this commercial. Dupes for on-air use are made and sent to the TV stations on the media schedule.

The foregoing is, of necessity, only a summary of events in the production of a TV or radio commercial. Details would fill a book at least the length of this one. But the summary should give you some indication of the enormous attention to detail, as well as the combination of creativity and craftsmanship, that so many people expend to make a commercial an effective selling tool.

Production Choices

It takes much less time to produce a commercial today than it did a few years ago. You can now shoot and finish a film commercial in a few days, instead of weeks. This increase in efficiency has been accomplished by the procedure of transferring film to videotape or computer disk for editing. For example, you can shoot film on Monday, have the film lab develop the negative that night, and transfer film to tape and start editing on Tuesday. By the end of the day, you can have a finished commercial. If you shoot on videotape, completion time can even be shorter. You can start editing immediately after the shoot. In fact, if you are shooting in a tape studio, you create the commercial in "real time." This means that you are actually editing as you go. When you are finished shooting, your commercial is ready.

Like production times, production costs vary greatly. But while the time necessary to shoot, process, and edit a TV spot has generally declined, costs have skyrocketed. Today, $1 million commercials are not at all uncommon. Yet, the majority of spots, even those produced at major production houses, cost considerably less. And, if you are working at a small agency for small-budget clients, you will probably produce commercials for less than $50,000, and perhaps for even less than $25,000. But whatever the budget, the commercial creator is responsible for making every client dollar do its job. And that job is to sell. Producing a commercial takes detailed planning. The better the planning up front, the fewer costly changes and corrections later on.

Besides deciding how much time you can afford to spend and how much money you can afford to invest in making your commercial, you must answer a number of other important questions. Will you shoot on location or in a studio? Will you use film or videotape? If you choose film, what size will be most effective and least costly? Whom will you select to perform, direct, and edit the commercial?

In addition, technical experts can provide you with a vast array of special effects: fancy opticals, wipes, dissolves, overlaps, fractionalized or split-screen units, prism shots, flash cuts, slow and fast motion—the list is almost endless.

You can take and retake sequences and then select the ones best qualified for your commercial. You can zero in with extreme microphotography. You can, as one golf ball spot did, start on a close-up of the ball and zoom back for what seems like a half a mile. You can use a narrow field of vision or a wide-angle lens. You can also pan, truck, go out of focus, or come into focus. In commercials that you create, you are limited only by your imagination, your production staff's ingenuity, and, of course, by your client's time and money.

Studio Shooting
Studios in major cities have complete facilities for photographing the most complex commercials. Studios range in size from small "insert" rooms used exclusively for close-up work (of packages, hands, labels, and so on), to animation studios in which drawings are photographed frame by frame, to the huge, arena-like sound stages in the Los Angeles area. Most of the latter belong to major feature-film studios, which often devote a large portion of their production schedules to the filming of TV programs and spots.

Reliable, creative production houses either have their own studios or rent space for shooting a commercial. These companies can be found in Canada, Mexico, and Puerto Rico and throughout Europe. Just as Hollywood is no longer the only center for feature films, it and New York City are no longer the only centers for the production of spots for television. A great deal of shooting is done in Orlando, Miami, and Toronto. Many agencies and clients use European studios for special scenes or special casting, not to mention production economies. Because the production field is extremely competitive, there is practically no limit to the effects you can ask for and get—budget permitting.

There are many good production houses in the smaller cities today. And, if you are working for a small client with a limited production budget, you may very well produce your commercial at the local television station. If this is the case, it is important to realize that you cannot do in Burlington, Iowa, what you might do in Hollywood. Understand the limitations of local low-budget production and plan your commercial accordingly. Keep it simple. Don't try for tricky effects. And don't assume you can find local talent that can pull off an outstanding slice-of-life commercial.

Location Shooting
More and more, commercials are being shot on location, for many good reasons. Improvement in film quality, ease of travel, wider use of off-beat camera techniques, and the compelling desire to look different from competition are some. But the overriding reason is authenticity or realism. For many commercials today, this demand practically necessities location shooting—even multilocation shooting is required in some cases.

For talent, production crew, agency staff, and client personnel to go on location, the budget must be generous and the objectives worthwhile.

Location shooting is costly, and it must be weighed against trying to achieve authenticity in a studio. Because of the colorful, authentic locales of feature films, viewers have grown accustomed to realism. And this quality in a commercial can add to the spot's believability.

Commercials for spaghetti are now filmed in Italy, the coffee-growing areas of Colombia are familiar TV sights, and Paris is a much-used backdrop for fashion and perfume spots. Airlines with overseas routes enhance their images by spotlighting foreign scenes, and orange juice commercials are shot on Florida beaches. All these locations are used for the realism they bring to the commercials.

As we have stated, motion pictures are, in part, responsible for this trend. Another stimulus has come from the flexibility of TV news programs, whose camera operators and reporters are all over the world. On-the-spot reports are filed every day and funneled into every TV home as a matter of course. Again, viewers have come to expect location shots from around the world.

Be guided by your objectives in deciding between studio and location. If location shooting will give you a more authentic-looking commercial for your product, make it show up on your storyboard. Perhaps you need a location only to set the stage for your message. If this is the case, your producer can obtain footage already in existence from a stock film company. Than you can shoot the balance of your commercial in close-ups in a studio—and save. You will also find that sometimes it is cheaper to go on location to get a shot than to build a set in a studio. For example, rather than build a set to show a woman shopping in a supermarket, shoot the scene in the local supermarket.

Live

Live commercials were the rule in the early days of television, even for network shows. From simplistic announcer-on-camera-holding-the-product to elaborate studio productions, live commercials, telecast as they were being performed, were sometimes exciting, usually frustrating, and often dull.

Every nuance, every light, every piece of business, props, letter-perfect actors—every detail of a live commercial had to be preplanned and re-hearsed. The comic history of television includes commercials that featured refrigerator doors that wouldn't open, dogs that refused pet food, cleansers that failed to wipe up dirt. No wonder film became the major medium for commercials!

Almost no commercials are done live today. The few that are, are on news and personality shows of local TV stations. Some network "talk-and-plug-my-latest-movie" shows have the host or announcer deliver the commercial, but these are the exceptions rather than the rule.

Creating a commercial for live delivery demands simplicity, mostly because your set will be restricting. The local station might have only one or two cameras. So you must plan your moves and dissolves and cuts carefully, allowing time for changing a lens or repositioning a camera. And you cannot expect to have carte blanche in sets or lighting or talent. Whatever titles you use may be art work, shown directly on camera, or translated into slides and fed into the system on cue by the director.

Videotape

The proponents of videotape argue that it has three basic advantages over film: less cost, a shorter production time, and more control in the studio—you can see what you are doing each step of the way.

Most people are unable to distinguish between a live telecast and one on videotape. Tape records electronically and plays back electronically for transmission; there is no perceptible loss of quality. Tape gives commercials a sense of "presence," which can be important to advertisers.

Speed is all-important to advertiser and agency. Tape is immediate because it requires no processing, whereas film must be developed, printed, and copied before it can be edited. A tape commercial can be completed in hours, whereas film can take weeks.

Tape also allows the entire production team to view "takes" immediately, make suggestions and improvements, and retake and view again. Reshooting with film means rerenting studio and equipment and calling back crew and performers.

If you want the viewer to feel that what he or she is seeing is happening at this moment, videotape will work. If it would be incredible to the viewer that what is seen is happening right now, you probably do not want the "live" look. And film may be your choice for this reason alone.

Can you shoot videotape and avoid the "live" look? Yes, if you light for film and use filters over the camera lens. So, wanting the "live" look is a reason to use videotape, but the "live" look can be avoided. And if you don't want it, you can still consider tape.

The "live" look works for an on-camera spokesperson commercial. The viewer can accept the idea that the spokesperson is at that moment in a television studio presenting the product story. The "live" look does not work for a slice-of-life commercial. The viewer cannot believe that he is at the moment viewing a family at their breakfast table solving the teenage eating problem with a particular brand of cereal. He or she will accept this contrivance in a little filmed drama. But if it looks "live," it will be rejected as implausible.

Can the viewer believe that what is seen could be happening right now? This is the basic question you should ask in order to determine if you want the "live" look. If appropriate, the "live" look is powerful. We are particularly interested in seeing what is happening right now.

Film

The proponents of film talk primarily about the beauty of the "film look." And there is little doubt that a creative cinematographer can give you a degree of nuance and subtlety in picture quality that is difficult if not impossible to achieve on videotape. There are certain subjects that almost demand this capability of film. A lovely model in a cosmetic commercial looks lovelier and softer on film. Outdoor scenic beauty is captured on film. Film can give your commercial a surreal quality, if that is what you want. Film is a more versatile medium than videotape in getting that special look.

Film has greater fidelity than tape. Whites are white, not light gray. Blacks are black, not dark gray. Colors are brighter, richer. Textures, shadows, and details are more discernable.

The best directors, the best cinematographers, the best production houses have traditionally worked in the film medium. However, this is less

true than it was a few years ago. And today most film people will also shoot tape, if you request it. Still, even today, the star directors and the creative production houses prefer the film medium and work best in it. This in itself may cause you to choose film.

Low cost has always been touted as a major advantage in shooting on videotape. If you are shooting a local commercial, and your production budget is small, videotape is less expensive than 35mm film. However, you may consider 16mm. It has been greatly improved in recent years. It gives you the "film" look at a cost comparable to tape.

Videotaping is faster. No film labs are involved. But shooting on film and finishing on tape or on disk are almost as fast.

When you shoot tape, you see on a monitor exactly what is recorded. However, a tape monitor can be rigged with a film camera so that you see on the monitor what the camera is seeing. And you can play it back after each take.

Of tape's three primary, if diminishing, advantages—speed, low cost, and seeing what you are getting—cost remains the most important determining factor in making the film-versus-tape decision. If it is a low-budget local spot, tape is still the answer. The choices include digital, one-inch, and Beta SP. High 8 and S-VHS tape are marginally acceptable. VHS is not acceptable.

If cost is not important, you will probably choose between film and tape on the basis of who you want to work with and the kind of "look" you want your commercial to have.

Film Color and Size

Your commercial structure and content will determine whether you shoot in a studio or on location and whether you use film or tape. It will also influence your producer and director in their choice of film size and color. A few years ago, almost no commercials were filmed in black and white; color was king. The reasoning was simple: color TV set owners expected to see color. Today, a commercial may be shot in black and white to create a certain mood. Or a spot may use both color *and* black and white. For instance, a commercial for Maalox antacid uses color to portray a man in the present day. Black and white flashbacks show him at the doctor's office.

The quality of film has improved enormously over the years. Tones, shading, and light value can be controlled to a fine degree. Experimentation has widened the range of effects available and made film an artistic medium of expression.

By carefully planning each scene, your director will include everything you want inside the safety area, the portion of film frame that does not include the TV cut-off zone. The TV cut-off zone is the area around the perimeter of a film frame that is not shown on a TV receiver. Everything inside its circumference will be seen on a TV receiver. Your action and titles must, of course, be placed within the area received by TV. Perhaps you have been made aware of this while viewing some old feature film that had titles stretched across the screen. All these would be seen in a theater, but the letters far left and far right are cut off on your home TV screen.

The narrower, smaller, 16mm frame is becoming more popular with commercial directors. It has been greatly improved in recent years and can provide a beautiful image. Sixteen millimeter film is easier to work with than 35mm, and the cameras for 16mm are lighter and more mobile. The film is less expensive to develop. But it has some restrictions. When 16mm is transferred to videotape or blown up to 35mm, it loses a percentage of pictorial clarity and intensity; it becomes less sharp.

However, 16mm is ideal for some commercials. Today, many spots are filmed in 16mm to acheive a reportorial, or cinema-vérité quality. Handheld cameras move, bounce, pan quickly, zoom in and out. Directors use this technique to gain and transmit a feeling of actuality, of realism and spontaneity. It can be extremely effective, all other facets of the commercial being equal.

Super 16 is "widescreen" 16mm. It has an aspect ratio almost identical to the proposed aspect ratio for High Definition TV (HDTV). This means that the super 16mm picture will fit almost perfectly into the TV screen of tomorrow. So 16mm will be easy to use in future commercials.

Casting

You have created a commercial. The storyboard has been approved and the budget has been signed. How do you and your producer make sure that your commercial will have spontaneity and vitality before you go to the studio to film it? By selecting your actors and announcers with care.

Announcers should be chosen for their voice qualities and the expressive way they read the copy. Actors should be chosen because they best express the characters in the commercial, not because they are fashion model pretty or handsome. An actor's projection of character and presence are the qualities to look for. Commercials must involve the viewer emotionally in order to create conviction—and sales. An actor must have conviction and express it spontaneously.

If you work in a small advertising agency, your producer and you will probably do the casting. Large agencies have casting directors on their staffs, usually persons with theatrical experience and entertainment world contacts.

It is absolutely essential that the casting director know precisely the mood and tone of your commercial as well as its objective. Explain your thoughts about the commercial as you discuss the storyboard. Your casting director will have files on all available actors and announcers, with pictures and lists of credits (plays, movies, and commercials that each actor has done). You will save time by going through the pictures the casting director selects before audition time. But be careful: Some of the pictures may have been taken and retouched years ago.

Auditions

The casting director will then call the actor through his or her agent and schedule a time spot for an audition. Time can be saved by scheduling actors to appear in ten-minute intervals at the audition room (a large room in your office, at the production house, or at an outside casting director's studio). Fifteen minutes is a more comfortable time allotment for announcers. This will give them the opportunity to go over the script by themselves in the outer waiting room. Also, make sure they have time during the audition to change or alter their reading to gain the special emphasis you want.

You should have a list of the people who will audition, with enough space on the page to write your comments about their audition performance.

When the talent appears and introductions are made, try to put the actor at ease. Even long-time professionals sometimes become nervous at auditions. After general comment or two, describe the product you are advertising, the commercial, and the specific character you want him or her to audition for. Give the actor a few moments to go over the storyboard or script and read the part aloud once or twice. Give suggestions, but do not correct with a reading of your own. Remember, you are hiring a professional who, with direction at rehearsal and on the set, will give a good characterization. Chances are, you will get a reading with nuances that you did not know were in the script.

If your commercial has two or more actors with a dialogue, audition them together so that you can note stature, mannerisms, and interactions. Write comments before the next actor or group of actors come into the room to audition. They will be a helpful jog to your memory in later discussions.

Don't waste time—yours or the actors'. Two or three readings should be enough to indicate an actor's proficiency and suitability. Be sure to be courteous and friendly, but professional with the actors. This will help build a good attitude on the set when you film your spot.

The auditions will be videotaped. This can be valuable to you when you cast a commercial. A taped audition is by no means a finished, polished example of an actor's or announcer's work, but it will give you an on-the-spot indication of how well he or she will perform in your commercial. It will do two more things: Taping can facilitate postaudition reviews with the producer and possibly the client. Also, the tape can be placed in the agency's archives for future casting sessions.

Perhaps your commercial is a testimonial that involves actual homemakers, mechanics, and so on, rather than professional actors. Where do

you find them? The fast and easy way is to hire a company that specializes in finding "real" people. Or you could keep a lookout at your product's point of purchase. Make note of each customer. A short interview with selected ones should tell you if you have a potential spokesperson for your product. Plan to invite your two or three top choices to the studio—just in case one "freezes" once the camera is turned on.

Talent Payment

Paying for the talent is the responsibility of the agency casting director and/or producer, but as a creator of commercials, you should know the varying scales. Talent payment and repayment (residuals) can add up to a large part of any commercial's budget. Obviously, 20 men and women, all on camera, all with lines, will be far more costly than two characters who have no lines. It is part of your job to know your talent costs before you go over the budget at the storyboard stage.

The Screen Actors Guild (SAG) represents actors who appear in filmed commercials. The American Federation of Television and Radio Artists (AFTRA) represents actors who appear in taped commercials. Most top-notch actors belong to both unions. Definite rates or scales of pay have been set for differing appearances in commercials. An actor appearing in spots shown on coast-to-coast networks receives more money than, say, an actor in a commercial shown only in a small local area. An actor who appears as a principal character in a spot receives more pay than another actor in the same spot who appears only as an "extra."

It is not necessary to give all the details about different pay scales here. Let us rather sum up with this guideline: In these cost-conscious times, it is an economic necessity to keep the number of actors in your commercials within the limits of the budget.

12

Testing the Commercial

By Patrick J. Kelly
Marketing Research Associates

The objective of any TV commercial testing service is to measure the ability of the commercial to sell, to be remembered, and to communicate. The need to know is accentuated by the size of the advertising budget invested in a campaign. With such a sizable investment at stake, it is advisable to know, beforehand, how a commercial will perform compared with another, either for the same product or for a competitor's product. The effectiveness of commercials varies widely.

Services have been established to find out where a specific commercial lies in the effectiveness spectrum. Following are brief descriptions of some of the leading testing services—how they operate and what they offer.

Gallup & Robinson, Inc.

Gallup & Robinson's system of television commercial evaluation provides three basic facilities: On-Air Syndicated Total Prime Time Television Research (TPT); On-Air Custom; and Theater Pre-Tests. The survey is based on interviews with approximately 3,300 men and women, 18 years of age or older, selected from telephone directories covering the Philadelphia area.

During the interview, last night's prime time program schedule is read, and the interviewee is asked to reconstruct his or her viewing pattern by half-hour segments. All viewers are exposed to brand-name cues selected from the viewer's total viewing pattern via a priority system that includes all client commercials, competitive commercials, and the necessary balance from an "all other" group.

Viewers claiming recall of any given commercial are asked a series of open-ended questions. The answers are recorded to determine proof of commercial registration (PCR), level of idea communication, and commercial persuasiveness. PCR scores are reported as a percentage of the available audience—men or women exposed to and asked about commercial exposure.

Because of increased participation and increased complexity in developing TV marketing strategies, some advertisers need tailor-made measurements. In response to this need, Gallup & Robinson has developed a measurement on individual programs whenever, wherever, and with whomever the advertiser pleases.

The On-Air Single Show Surveys provide delayed, aided recall measurements using telephone interviewing. The service is available in 24 areas across the country, and additional markets can be added if needed. The basic reports developed are Proved Commercial Registration (PCR) and verbatim playback profiles leading to data on idea communication and buying attitudes.

For advertisers who want to pretest commercials, an in-theater testing arrangement is available. A sample of respondents is invited to attend a theater to view a TV program. After viewing the program, they are questioned about the program and television in general—nothing is said about the commercial spliced into the film. The day following exposure, the respondents are interviewed by telephone to obtain recall levels and idea communication and favorable buying attitude effectiveness data.

Burke Marketing Research, Inc.

The standard Burke technique involves telephone interviews the day after the commercial was aired, using the aided recall method and reflecting normal in-the-home viewing situations.

The usual sample size is 200 viewers of the test program, which yields a Commercial Audience (those who were actually in the room with the set, not asleep and not changing channels at the time of the test commercial exposure) of approximately 150, varying slightly in either direction, depending on the type of program. Tests using other sample sizes can be arranged.

Respondents are those who claim to have watched the program on which the test commercial was telecast. Interviewing times are flexible, so that the interviewers can best reach the particular audience segment desired.

The following timetable is standard for most Burke "dayafter" recall tests:

Flash scores, claimed and related recall, percentaged on Commercial Audience, are reported by telephone during the morning of the day following the test. These rapidly computed scores are usually accurate within one or two percentage points, but are confirmed within about three more days. Friday, Saturday, and Sunday tests are flash-reported on the following Monday.

One hundred percent of the related and unrelated verbatims, coded and uncoded, can be available about five days after the date of interviewing. Final reports are available between three and four weeks from date of interviewing.

The standard report contains, basically, three items of decision-making information:

1. A quantitative measure of the communication's effectiveness.

2. A coded and categorized summary of all that was remembered about the commercial.

3. A verbatim transcription of the playback from every respondent recalling anything about the commercial.

Additionally, Burke maintains a file of normative data against which recall scores for a specific study may be compared. Current normative data show mean averages, ranges, and bar graph distributions of claimed and related scores by length of commercial, product category, and sex.

Schwerin Research Corp.

Central to the Schwerin Research Corp. system is the assumption that advertising's ability to persuade consumers to prefer a given brand over its competition is the key indicator of effectiveness. Based on this assumption, several measures have been developed to reflect this position.

The Standard Service includes the Competitive Preference Score, Persuasibility Index, Brand Identification (Unaided), and Unaided Recall and Involvement. To supplement the basic standard measure, Schwerin Research has developed a variety of "diagnostic" measurements to assist in understanding the influence underlying advertising effectiveness—the Extended Service.

The technique used by Schwerin to measure the effectiveness of television advertising centers on a test audience in a test theater. A randomly selected panel views a "pilot" TV film interspersed with TV commercials.

The test audience is selected from telephone directories covering the geographical area surrounding a particular test center. Although the total audience on a given night represents a cross-section of the population 16 years of age or older and test data are obtained from the entire audience, the sample may be redefined after the fact so that test results for a particular product are based only on relevant consumers—namely, the analytical sample.

Following the introductory warm-up where the test director outlines the purpose of the session and gives instructions—but before exposure to any stimulus has taken place—the audience is offered the chance to win some prizes. In order to qualify for a prize, every respondent is asked to complete a ballot by checking the particular brand he or she would like to receive as a prize. Several product categories are included, and within each are listed the principal competing brands. Tickets are drawn on stage and the winner is given the product he or she selected.

This technique stimulates real buying behavior and provides data for the "Pre-Choice Measurement."

The audience is then shown the pilot program and three commercials (for one of the brands in each of the "Pre-Choice" checklists). The same pilot program is repeated from session to session to eliminate this element as a variable.

At the conclusion of the program, measures of "Unaided Recall" and "Brand Identification" are obtained, followed by the "Post-Choice Measurement," which is developed in the same manner as the "Pre-Choice" brand selections and drawings.

Summarization of the brand selections made after exposure to the test advertisement provides data for the "Post-Choice" percentages. These reflect the proportions of consumers favorably disposed toward a brand after exposure to a commercial for a brand in that category. The "Post-Choice" information serves as the final ingredient for the overall effectiveness measure.

Next, the involvement measure is obtained, followed by a short audience discussion about the program. For Extended Service Tests, the advertisement is again shown—out of program context—allowing for the special diagnostic questioning.

AdTel, Ltd.

The AdTel technique uses a dual-cable CATV system and two balanced purchase diary panels of 1,200 households each. The system has been wired using two cables, thus permitting wiring of panel homes to either cable to provide an alternate A and B checkerboard distribution.

AdTel can cut in test commercials to the B homes, while the A homes continue to get normal ad exposure. The corporate client must own the time—network or spot—into which the test commercial is cut. A client can have an unlimited number of cut-ins made without paying any cut-in charge.

Two matched panels are maintained—one for each cable. Panel families are personally recruited and trained. They must record all their food, drug, and other appropriate purchases in a weekly diary.

In addition to purchase information, the dairy contains a symptom section that enables AdTel

to measure low incidence health care products based on usage. A household reports the number of times each brand was taken by family members for various symptoms—headache, stomach ache, cold, cough, and so on. This information makes it possible for a manufacturer to test a campaign against a specific usage.

Panel members receive points for completing their weekly diaries. These points are redeemable for merchandise from a well-known mail-order catalog. These, together with other incentives, total about $100 a year for the average family.

To substantiate the written reports, AdTel conducts quarterly pantry and medicine chest audits. These records are compared by computer against dairy-reported purchases. This follow-up check helps to impress panelists that AdTel wants complete and accurate diary entries.

Data from the purchase diaries are processed into a four-week report. For each brand specified by the client, shares of unduplicated families purchasing, units, dollars, volume in ounces or another common denominator, and percentage of deal volume are shown.

In addition, a client receives a raw deck of data cards (or tape) covering every diary-recorded transaction in the product categories desired. These data enable the client to track such factors as trial and repeat, brand switching, the demographics of triers, users, and switchers, the importance of dealing, and so on.

AdTel also conducts three attitude and awareness studies throughout the year among people on the cable but not on the panel. These studies are diagnostic rather than definitive and can help guide analysis of the diary panel data.

Milwaukee Advertising Laboratory

The Milwaukee Advertising Laboratory is a research facility that provides a set of controlled conditions in a natural setting, within which the sales effectiveness of newspaper, Sunday supplement, direct mail, and television advertising can be measured without disturbing a current marketing program.

Two matched markets were developed by taking the four counties comprising the Greater

Milwaukee Market and dividing them into 104 newspaper circulation districts with about 2,500 newspaper subscribers in each. These were then split into two equal and matched markets of 52 districts each. From these two markets, probability samples of 750 families each are drawn.

Newspaper advertising reaching these two matching markets is controlled on a split-run and split distribution basis. Television advertising is controlled through the use of an electronic muter installed in all of the TV sets of the two samples. With the muter in use, it is possible to blank out a set of commercials from one group, while the other group receives the message. The television set simply goes blank, as does the sound, for the interim of the commercial but then returns to "live" for the program.

To collect the needed information, the Laboratory uses a consumer purchase diary. Each homemaker in each sample is asked to send in a weekly diary of all branded merchandise bought during the week. The homemaker is told how to do this during a basic placement interview.

To compensate the homemaker for cooperating, the Laboratory provides free maintenance service on all TV sets in the household as long as the householder participates as a panel member. Also, the householder can earn merchandise prizes from points earned by continued cooperation.

The weekly diaries are processed by computer, and printouts are sent directly to subscribing advertisers and their agencies. The reports show the total number of units bought in the product category, the distribution of brand shares by units, and the percentage in each market separately. Parallel reports cover total dollar sales by brand, total sales volume by brand, and additional data on how dealing affects volume each month.

Commercial Testing Service

Two types of measurements to appraise the performance of television commercials are offered by Commercial Testing Service: an evaluative measure and a diagnostic measure.

The evaluative measures are related to how well the commercial succeeds in building consumer acceptance and interest in the advertised brand. In addition to the overall measure of the effectiveness, CTS also offers measures defined by demographic characteristics (age, education, and so on), by product usage characteristics (heavy versus light users), and by brand attitude or brand usage segments.

The diagnostic measures are designed to appraise the content and execution of the commercial, including analysis of the points communicated and the extent to which the commercial message is considered important, believable, interesting, or involving.

Invitations to serve on a panel are mailed to residents living within a four- to six-mile radius of a suburban theater where the research session will be held. The invitation offers an opportunity to express opinions on television programs and commercials and states that door prizes will be awarded, along with additional incentives for attendance and cooperation.

Respondents are given a questionnaire to rate a number of brands in a number of product categories, using a five-point attitude scale. They are then shown a film that they are told is being considered for TV. Within the film are four commercials for noncompeting brands in some but not all of the product categories for which the respondents had previously indicated brand ratings. After screening, they are given a second questionnaire with several questions about the film. Then they are told that there will be a series of drawings and that the prizes will be a specified number of units of the product. They are asked to indicate how many of each of a restricted list of competitive brands they would like to win if their name is drawn. Obviously, the respondent would tend to indicate more of the brand most preferred.

A third questionnaire for each commercial contains a number of open-ended questions designed to provide information for diagnostic tabulation. It is also possible to include the client's own questions in this questionnaire.

The principal measure provided shows the gain or loss in buying interest caused by advertising exposure. Respondent attitude toward the various brands is predicted on the number of each brand indicated in the prize-drawing procedure. This ranking compared with the attitude recorded to test advertising indicates the effectiveness of the commercial.

13

Public Service Advertising

At a joint meeting of the American Association of Advertising Agencies and the Association of National Advertisers held at Hot Springs, Virginia, in 1941, James Webb Young—then at the J. Walter Thompson agency, but also a professor at the University of Chicago, a farmer in New Mexico, and a philosopher always—delivered a landmark speech in which he said: "Advertising is the most modern, streamlined, high speed means of communication plus persuasion yet invented by man. Because it is this, it has potentialities far beyond its present levels. It ought to be used extensively by governments, by political parties, by labor unions, by farm organizations, by the National Association of Manufacturers, by the great philanthropic foundations, by churches, and by universities. It ought to be used…in international relations, to create understanding and reduce friction. It ought to be used to wipe out such diseases of ignorance as childbed fever. It ought to do the nutritional job this country needs to have done. It ought to be the servant of music, of art, of literature and of all the forces of righteousness even more than it is."

The elevation of advertising to this new level of usefulness and public purpose as espoused by Mr. Young in 1941 has continued to this day under the aegis of The Advertising Council, headquartered in New York City, which operates wholly on a voluntary basis. The Advertising Council is a private, nonprofit organization consisting of advertising, business, and media people who have contributed billions of dollars in cre-ative time and advertising to promote improvement in such areas as better health, traffic safety, equal employment opportunity, forest fire prevention, and other vital concerns that affect the general public. Public service advertising is designed to move ideas instead of products, to get something done that needs to be done, and to support human needs and aspirations.

The products of the Council cover four broad areas: (1) developing human resources to improve people's lives, (2) promoting citizen awareness of health and other issues, (3) preserving natural resources, and (4) strengthening the economy. The following list, showing the wide and diverse range of public service causes that can be promoted through broadcast commercials of this nature, indicates some of the many areas in which the Advertising Council has served as the coordinator of promotional efforts:

- AIDS awareness

- Aid to higher education

- American Red Cross

- Alcoholism treatment

- Child abuse prevention

- Energy conservation

- High blood pressure education

- International Youth Exchange

- Mothers Against Drunk Driving

- National Organization on Disability

- Peace Corps

- Religion in American life

- United Negro College Fund

- United States Savings Bonds

Public service commercials on radio and tele-vision can and do use most of the formats dis-cussed in Chapter 3. No matter which format they employ, however, the appeal is frequently to the emotions. It is difficult to be unemotional about deaths caused by disease or drunk driving, abused or missing children, or the destruction of our environment.

The commercials on the following pages are outstanding examples of public service adver-tising.

Exhibit 13–1. Public Service: Drunk Driving Campaign (TV)

Advertiser: U.S. Department of Transportation

Agency: Wells Rich Greene BDDP

Product: National Highway Safety

Title: "Alex"/"Miranda"

Format: Slice-of-Life/Announcer

Length: 30 seconds

"ALEX" :30 CNTD - 5430 (CC)

WOMAN VO: Who is that swimming?
ALEX: I'm swimming.

WOMAN VO: Try to get your legs up.
ALEX: Like this?

WOMAN VO: That's the way, What'ya doing? Where's your kickin, Al? –That's it.

Alex Bishop.

ALEX: I'm almost there.
WOMAN: Okay.

Alex Bishop.
Killed by a drunk driver on November 8, 1992 on Kent-Kangley Road in Kent, Washington.

ALEX VO: I'm almost there, Mommy. I'm almost there.

WOMAN VO: Whoa. You made it all the way.
ANNCR VO: If you won't stop your friend from driving drunk,

who will?
WOMAN VO: Now what're you doing? –Good job.

FRIENDS DON'T LET FRIENDS DRIVE DRUNK.

Ad Council   U.S. Department of Transportation

ANNCR VO: Do whatever it takes.
WOMAN VO: Are you having a good time?
ALEX VO: Yeah.

"MIRANDA" :30 CNTD - 5530 (CC)

CHORUS SINGING VO: ...BIRTHDAY TO YOU. HAPPY BIRTHDAY TO YOU.

HAPPY BIRTHDAY, DEAR MIRANDA. GOD BLESS YOU.

HAPPY BIRTHDAY TO YOU.

Miranda Fay Standiford.

(SFX: CLAPPING, CHEER-ING)

Miranda Fay Standiford.
Killed by a drunk driver on May 1, 1994 on Highway 60 in Borden, Indiana.

WOMAN VO: Do you need some scissors or something?

ANNCR VO: If you don't stop your friend from driving drunk, who will?

FRIENDS DON'T LET FRIENDS DRIVE DRUNK.

Ad Council   U.S. Department of Transportation

Do whatever it takes.

Exhibit 13–2. Public Service: Drunk Driving (Radio)

Advertiser: U.S. Department of Transportation   **Title:** "Miranda/Alex Combo"
Agency: Wells Rich Greene BDDP   **Format:** Slice-of-Life/Announcer
Product: National Highway Safety   **Length:** 60 seconds

SFX:	(MUSIC UNDER) (WE HEAR MIRANDA AND HER FAMILY SINGING "HAPPY BIRTHDAY")
ANNCR:	This is from the video of Miranda Standiford's 3rd birthday party. (MUSIC AND SINGING CONTINUES)
ANNCR:	Not long after this was recorded, Miranda was killed by a drunk driver. (BACKGROUND PARTY SOUND CONTINUES)
ANNCR:	Do whatever it takes. Friends don't let friends drive drunk.
SFX:	(SOUND FADE OUT AND UP ON ALEX SEGMENT) (WE HEAR ALEX BISHOP AND HIS MOM IN A POOL, TEACHING ALEX HOW TO SWIM)
ANNCR:	This is from a video of Alex Bishop, 5 years old, learning to swim. (BACKGROUND SOUND CONTINUES)
ANNCR:	Not long after this was recorded, Alex was killed by a drunk driver. (BACKGROUND SOUND CONTINUES)
ANNCR:	Do whatever it takes. Friends don't let friends drive drunk. An appeal from the Ad Council, the Department of Transportation, and this station. (BACKGROUND SOUND OUT)

Exhibit 13–3. Public Service: AIDS Prevention (TV)

Advertiser: U.S. Department of Health &
Human Services

Title: "Self Realization"

Agency: Della Femina, McNamee, WCRS

Format: Animation

Product: AIDS Prevention

Length: 60 seconds

(MUSIC UNDER)
JEANINE: Jeanine woke up

in a cold sweat, with one thing echoing through her brain.

"Who was this guy in her bathroom?"

BARRY: Meanwhile, Barry was thinking,

"Whose bathroom am I in?"

JEANINE: Jeanine remembered going to the party the night before and getting smashed out of her mind.

BARRY: Barry remembered getting drunk and acting really stupid.

JEANINE: Eventually...
BARRY: The whole evening came back.

JEANINE: Oh, I must be really stupid.

BARRY: I must be really dumb.

JEANINE: What did I do? How did I get myself into this?

BARRY: What did I do? How did I get myself into this?

JEANINE: What about...
BARRY: What about...
BOTH: What about AIDS?

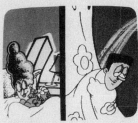

JEANINE: Then they both realized, much to their relief, that unlike the rest of us...
BARRY: ...they were just cartoons.

JEANINE: GET HIGH.
BARRY: GET STUPID.
JEANINE: GET AIDS.

GET HIGH
GET STUPID
GET AIDS

FOR MORE INFORMATION CALL:
1-800-662-HELP

NATIONAL INSTITUTE ON DRUG ABUSE   AD COUNCIL   U.S. DEPARTMENT OF HEALTH AND HUMAN SERVICES

Exhibit 13–4. Public Service: AIDS Prevention (Radio)

Advertiser: American Foundation for AIDS Research/National AIDS Network

Title: "Reasons"

Agency: Della Femina, McNamee, WCRS

Format: Testimonial/Announcer

Product: AIDS Prevention

Length: 60 seconds

SFX: TRAFFIC NOISES UNDER INITIAL VOICES

MAN: They kinda cramp my style.

MAN: It's embarrassing to buy them.

MAN: It's just not the same, y' know.

WOMAN: I'm afraid to bring it up, 'cause I'm worried my boyfriend'll get turned off.

WOMAN: It can sound like you don't trust him.

MAN: I mean, they're not the most romantic things in the world, are they?

ANNCR: There are a million reasons for not using condoms, none of them as good as the reason you should. Because if you're going to have sex, a latex condom with spermicide is your best protection against the AIDS virus: a virus that's already responsible for more than 30,000 American deaths. And that number will almost double in just the next few years. Because there is no cure for AIDS. You can't walk into a store, buy some medicine, and get over it. But you can walk into a store, buy some latex condoms, and use them. After all, using a condom won't kill you; not using one, might.

ANNCR: A public service message from the American Foundation for AIDS Research, the National AIDS Network, and the Ad Council. Use condoms according to manufacturers' directions.

Exhibit 13-5. Public Service: Domestic Violence (TV)

Advertiser: Family Violence Prevention Fund
Agency: Altschiller Reitzfeld
Product: Domestic Violence Prevention

Title: "Neighbors"
Format: Slice-of-Life/Announcer
Length: 60 seconds

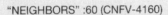

"NEIGHBORS" :60 (CNFV-4160)

Also available in :30 length, CNFV-4130

SOUNDS OF VIOLENT
DOMESTIC FIGHT OVERHEAD
(SFX: CRASH)

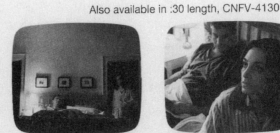

(SFX: WOMAN CRIES)

(SFX: BANGING)
(WOMAN SCREAMS)

(SFX: WOMAN CRIES)

(SFX: FIGHT CONTINUES)

(SFX: LIGHT CLICKS OFF)

IT IS YOUR BUSINESS.

(CRYING FADES TO SILENCE)

THERE'S **NO** EXCUSE
1-800-777-1960
Family Violence Prevention Fund

ANNCR VO: For information
about how you can help stop
domestic violence, call us.

"WEDDING" :15 (CNFV-4115)

Also available in :10 length, CNFV-4110

(SFX: ORGAN MUSIC & CLICK
OF STROBE FLASH
THROUGHOUT)

ANNCR VO: 42% of all
murdered women are killed
by men...

who promised to love them.

THERE'S **NO** EXCUSE
for Domestic Violence.
1-800-777-1960
Family Violence Prevention Fund

Help stop domestic violence.
Call us.

Exhibit 13–6. Public Service: Domestic Violence (Radio)

Advertiser: Family Violence Prevention Fund **Title:** "Neighbors"
Agency: Altschiller Reitzfeld **Format:** Sound Effects/Announcer
Product: Domestic Violence Prevention **Length:** 60 seconds

SFX: Throughout spot, sounds of a vicious fight between a man and a women are heard. Sounds and words are muffled, but it is clear that a woman is being abused.

ANNCR: At one time or another, most of us have seen a woman abused. Sometimes you only hear it. From a neighbor's apartment or out in the street. (SFX UP)
Domestic violence just isn't right. You want to stop it, but it's none of your business, right? (SFX UP)
You don't want to get involved. It's just a private thing. (SFX UP)
But, if someone were playing music too loud, you'd do something. (SFX UP)
Every nine seconds, another woman is beaten. Every nine seconds. For information about how you can help stop domestic violence, call us at 1-800-777-1960. This public service message was brought to you by the Family Violence Prevention Fund and the Ad Council.

Glossary

Radio

Account A sponsor who has entered into a contract with a station or network; also a contract between a sponsor and an advertising agency or representative.

Across the board A program presented five days a week at the same time each day.

Ad-lib To announce or talk without a prepared script.

AFTRA American Federation of Television and Radio Artists. A national labor organization representing people in radio and television, especially performers (talent).

Aircheck A recording of a program or commercial.

Airshift Or "show" time—when talent is on the air.

Allocation The specific assignment of frequency and power to a station by the Federal Communication Commission.

Audition The testing, usually in a studio, of talent for a particular role in a commercial or a performance.

Back-timing Timing the ending stories of a newscast, speech, or music, and so on, in a program to enable the talent to get off the air on time.

Block programming The scheduling of programs of similar appeal back-to-back to keep listeners from switching to another station.

Board The control panel through which the broadcast program passes.

Bulletin The first brief announcement of an important news event.

Call letters Initials assigned by the Federal Communication Commission to identify a station.

Cart A cassette-type cartridge. Used for taped announcements, jingles, commercials, music, or bridges, and so on.

Clearing music Obtaining releases (approval) from the copyright holders of music, or ascertaining whether the station, as a result of contracts with organizations holding copyrights (ASCAP, BMI) is privileged to present a musical selection.

Close The closing announcement to a program.

Cluster buster A line or phrase to break up back-to-back commercial announcements.

Commentary A selection of a program devoted to opinion.

Commercial Advertising; sometimes called a "spot."

Continuity writer One who creates radio copy other than news.

Cue A signal, either verbal or by sign.

Cut a record To make a recording or transcription; also, "make a tape" or "lay down a tape."

Dateline program A news program written in bulletin style with each story beginning with the name of the city or location in which the story originated.

Dead air   Unintentional silence on air.

DGA   Directors Guild of America. A national organization representing film, television, and radio directors.

Drive time   Those morning and late-afternoon hours when commuters are driving to and from work.

Dub or dubbing   Transferring material from one record or tape to another.

Fade   A decrease in volume.

Fading in   Increasing volume so that music, sound, or speech rises in volume gradually.

Feedback   The return of sound from a loud-speaker to the microphone in which it originated; also, public response to station management either in complaint or praise.

Feeding   The delivery of a program over a telephone hookup either to a network or some other point.

Fluff   A mistake in delivery by talent.

Format   The type of programming a station uses (for example, classical music, all news, top forty, MOR, beautiful music).

Frequency discount   A discount given by a network or station to a sponsor who buys commercial time in large quantities.

Fuzzy   Applies to program or line that is not clear.

Gain   Control of volume; usually called "riding gain."

Guideline   A one-word description of a news story. Also called "slug" or "slugline."

I.D.   Station call letters followed by location (for example, WBCB Levittown-Fairless Hills).

Independent station   A local, commercial station not affiliated with any network, usually found in the larger markets.

Jingle   A musical commercial for a product, service, or station.

Jumping cue   When an announcer or newscaster starts a program before he or she is scheduled to begin.

Level   The volume noted on the meter (potentiometer) of the control board. A knob sometimes called a "pot."

Line   A telephone line (wire) used for the transmission of a program.

Live announcement   A message read in person, not prerecorded.

Live mike   A microphone that is turned on.

Log   A record or schedule of everything broadcast; required by the FCC.

Monitoring   Listening to a program.

MOR   A format used by many stations featuring "middle-of-the-road" type music.

NAB   National Association of Broadcasters. A trade organization devoted to promoting radio and TV stations.

NABET   National Association of Broadcast Engineers and Technicians. A labor organization.

News analyst   One who reports, analyzes, and comments on news.

Newscaster   One who reads straight news on the air and who may or may not write his or her own news for on-air delivery.

News editor   One who rewrites, edits, and supervises the news program. May also deliver news on the air.

O & O stations   Broadcasting stations "owned and operated" by a network. Usually very successful stations in large markets that contribute handsomely to a network's total profit.

Open   An introductory announcement to a program.

Optional copy   Additional news items that announcer or newscaster can use if he or she runs short of copy.

Overmodulating   Putting too much volume over the air; sometimes called "blasting."

Participating sponsor   A client who shares commercial time with other sponsors of the same program.

PBS   Public Broadcasting System. A nonprofit radio and TV network.

Protection   An extra take, to be used in case the selected take is ruined or lost.

PSA   A public service announcement.

Public domain   (or PD) Program or commercial content not protected by copyright that may be used freely without payment of a fee. PD can also mean program director.

RAB   Radio Advertising Bureau.

Ratings Statistical measurements of a station's audience.

Reading cold Reading a program or a news story on the air without having rehearsed it.

Release Copy sent in advance to be held for use at a designated time.

Remote A program picked up from outside the studio (for example, football games, reports from the scene of a fire or flood).

Rewrite A news story or program that undergoes revision.

RTNDA Radio-Television News Directors Association.

Special event On-the-scene broadcast of a news event, usually planned.

Spot A commercial, either recorded or delivered live.

Standby A program used in emergencies.

Stand by A cue to performers before they are given a live microphone.

Station break Or just "break." A pause to permit local stations to identify themselves.

Sustainer A program that is not sponsored.

Tack-up A news program prepared by pasting or stapling wire copy to sheets of copy paper and then editing the stories.

Take A performance attempt. When recording, each attempt is given a number—"Take One," "Take Two," and so on. The take deemed most satisfactorily is then used.

Talk-over When an announcer talks during the first few bars of a musical selection.

Ticket A license granted by the FCC.

Time copy Copy for news or a live commercial that is back-timed.

Traffic A station or network department receives orders for commercials, makes certain that they get on the air, and then follows up in billing advertisers.

Triple-spotting Running three separate commercials in one commercial time period.

Wire copy News, sports, weather, and information originating from the Associated Press, United Press International, or another news service.

Woof The sound made by an engineer into a microphone to synchronize audio levels.

Television

AAAA American Association of Advertising Agencies, or the 4 A's. A national organization of advertising agencies devoted to standardizing procedures and upgrading the business level of its members.

Above the line Motion picture, television, or radio costs relating to artistic or creative elements in production (writing, acting, directing, music, and so on). (Compare with *below the line*.)

Abstract set A nonrepresentational setting using elements such as drapes, columns, steps, platforms, free-standing flats with various textures and geometrical forms, and so on. Such a setting has no definite locale, but may suggest one.

Academy field Looking through the lens of a motion picture camera, one sees two sets of lines framing the rectangular scene. The larger represents what will be seen when the film is projected on a regular screen; this is "academy field" or "academy framing." The smaller set of lines defines the TV field (or "TV cutoff") and shows what will appear on the TV screen. In filming a TV commercial, all essential elements in a scene should be confined to the smaller area.

Academy leader On a TV commercial print or other film print, the section of film with a series of "countdown" numbers to enable the projectionist to cue the opening scene or title of the picture.

Account executive The person at an advertising agency who coordinates all other agency professionals on an account and acts as a liaison between agency and client.

Across the board A show that airs at the same time five days a week. So called because it appears straight across the program board each of the first five days.

Action Any movement that takes place in front of a camera or on film. Any movement that carries the story forward and develops the plot.

A.D. Abbreviation for assistant director; a member of the production crew who handles details relating to the actual shooting of a commercial, such as cast and crew calls, adherence to production schedules, and so on.

Adjacencies Commercials or programs that immediately precede or follow one another.

Ad-lib To extemporize lines or music not written into the script or the musical score.

ADO The brand name of one type of electronic special effects device.

Advertising Council The joint body of the AAAA and the ANA (Association of National Advertisers) and media, through which public service projects are developed and channeled to advertisers for their support (for example, Smokey the Bear, Cancer Crusade).

Affiliate A television or radio station associated by contract with a network.

AFTRA Abbreviation for American Federation of Television and Radio Artists, a member of AFL, made up of actors, singer, announcers, and so on. It is concerned with commercials made on videotape and regulates wage scales for its members. The Screen Actors Guild (SAG) serves the same function for talent appearing in filmed commercials. Many performers belong to both unions.

Aided recall A research interviewing technique in which the respondent is given a hint or reminder to elicit a meaningful response. The opposite of this is a "free response" in which the person being interviewed is not given a hint.

Aircheck A recording, either audio or video, or both, of an actual broadcast. It serves as a file copy of a program or commercial for an agency, a sponsor, or a competitive sponsor.

Alternate sponsorship When two advertisers share a single program with one advertiser dominant one week and the other the following week (or whenever the programs are scheduled).

Analog Recording, whether audio or video, that makes an approximate copy of the original. See *digital*.

Angle of view The amount of horizontal area of a scene that registers on a lens. Varies in proportion to size of lens, from narrow to wide angle.

Angle shot A camera shot taken from any position except straight on the subject.

Animatic A test commercial that is a series of still drawings that are dissolved together to create a rough approximation of movement.

Animation Creating an illusion of motion by photographing a series of drawings so that the drawings appear to move. Usually done in a cartoon style. Sometimes combined with live action on film.

Animation stand A piece of equipment that supports a camera above animation cells and can move the camera in a very precise way. An animation stand is also used for animatics, titling, and sometimes for a product shot if the product is relatively flat, such as a magazine.

Announcement spot A brief commercial not integrated into the program.

Announcer (1) The member of a radio or television station staff assigned the duty of introducing and describing program features; (2) the station staff member who delivers a commercial live; (3) the talent who delivers the commercial message (or part of it) either on camera or as a voice-over.

Arc A strong, blue-white light that glows as a result of electricity sparking across two carbon electrodes (as opposed to a filament that glows from heat).

Arri Nickname for an Arriflex camera, 35mm, widely used in making filmed commercials.

Art Director The person who, together with the copywriter, generates a concept for a commercial and draws the pictures on the storyboard. In production, the art director works with the set designer, wardrobe and hair and makeup, the director of photography, and the director, to help achieve the desired "look" to the production.

ASCAP American Society of Composers, Authors and Publishers; a music-licensing organization.

Audience accumulation An increase in audience achieved by broadcasting a program in a series rather than just once.

Audience composition A term that refers to a classification of the individuals or the households in a television or radio audience into various categories. Common categories for individuals are age and sex groupings (men, women, teenagers, and children). Common categories for households are based on the number of members of the household, age or education of the head of the household, household income, and so forth.

Audience flow   The statistical composition of the total audience of a program showing the parts: (1) retained from the previous program, (2) transferred from another station, and (3) tuned in for the first time.

Audience profile   A demographic description of the people exposed to a program or commercial.

Audience share   The number or proportion of all home sets in use that are tuned to a particular program.

Audimeter   An electric rating research device. This device is used by the A.C. Nielsen Co. to record the radio and TV tuning of sets in selected homes.

Audio   The sound portion of a TV broadcast.

Audition   A tryout of actors, announcers, musicians, or programs.

Availability   In broadcasting, a time period available for purchase by an agency for an advertiser. For talent, the word is used to refer to the artist's lack of conflict either in a product category or for a recording or shooting date.

Average audience rating   A type of rating computed for some specified interval of time, such as for the length of a television or radio program or for a 15- or 30-minute period.

Avid   The brand name of a system for nonlinear, random-access computer editing.

Background   A broadcasting sound effect, musical or otherwise, used behind or under the dialogue or other program elements. In TV storyboards, the letters "'BG" refer to the setting behind the actors, figures, or products in the foreground.

Back light   Illumination from behind the subject and opposite the camera.

Back lot   In a large studio, where temporary exterior sets are constructed, or where there are permanent exterior sets that recreate extensive areas, such as a New York street scene, an Old West town, etc.

Back to back   A broadcast situation in which two or more commercials directly follow each other without a break. Also called "piggyback."

Balop   Generally, any opaque projector or the slides and art work prepared for it. The projector consists of (1) an illuminated stage or surface to hold the object to be televised and (2) a lens placed to project the image on the tube in the pickup camera. Multistage balops permit dissolves, superimpositions, and simple animation.

Balopticon (balops)   A type of television animation made possible through the use of a Balopticon machine, usually in a TV station.

Basic network   The section of a national television or radio network covering the more populous markets.

BCU   (TCU, ECU) An extremely narrow angle picture. Big close-up. Tight close-up. Extreme close-up.

Below the line   Motion picture, television, or radio costs relating to the technical or material elements in production (props, sets, equipment, staging services, and so on).

Billboard   An announcement at the beginning of a broadcast that lists the sponsor and/or products featured in the program.

Bit   A small part in a television program or commercial.

Blowup   A scene that has been enlarged.

Book   To hire an actor to appear in a commercial.

Bridge   Music or sound effect linking two scenes in a TV or radio program.

Business   An actor's movement, especially with props; action used to add interest to a program or commercial.

Busy   Describes a setting or background that is too elaborate, thereby diverting the viewer's attention from the actors or object that should predominate.

Buyout   Compensation for a performer not according to the prevailing scale with residual benefits, but in one complete and final sum.

Call letters   Initials assigned by the Federal Communications Commission to identify a station.

Camera angle Any various ways of positioning a camera, vertically and horizontally.

Camera rehearsal Similar to a dress rehearsal in stage vernacular, in which all talent is present and in costume and the complete production is shot by the camera operator for a final check before shooting film.

Casting profile A description of the role(s) to be played in a commercial.

Channel A band of radio frequencies assigned to a given radio or TV station, or assigned to other broadcasting purposes.

Cheat To take creative license with some aspect of film production. For example, when four people are seated at a dinner table in real life, they might be at right angles facing due north, south, east, and west. On camera, they would be in a semicircle facing east, southeast, southwest, and west. The actors cheat the seating arrangement so that the camera does not shoot the back of anybody's head.

Chyron The brand name of an electronic title and super generator.

Cinematographer See director of photography.

Cinema vérité A style of filming that tries to create absolute reality by attempting to break down the imaginary "stage" that separates the camera and its subject. In cinema vérité, the camera is usually hand held, it moves to whoever is speaking without cutting, and the lights, camera, and crew may at some point be in the scene.

Circulation The number of households or individuals, regardless of where located, that are estimated to be in the audience of a given television or radio network or station at least once during some specified period of time (for example, one week or one month). Thus, circulation is simply a term used to describe the size of the cumulative audience of a network or a station over some period of time.

Class (A, B, C) rates The charges or fees for different segments on a TV or radio station. The most desirable and costly TV time is usually between 6:00 and 11:00 p.m. Rates vary from city to city and from station to station.

Claymation A type of stop motion animation in which flexible clay puppets are moved slightly each time the camera shoots a frame or two.

Clear (1) To obtain legal permission from responsible sources to use a musical selection, photograph, film clip, or quotation in an advertisement. (2) to arrange for approval from a station for a certain time slot for a program or commercial.

Close-up A shot of an individual with the camera moved in close so that the head and shoulders fill the screen. A big close-up (BCU) may include only the head or perhaps just the eyes. A close-up shot (CU) may also be taken of an object.

Closed circuit A television program that is distributed to specific television receivers but not telecast to the public.

CMX The brand name of a master control unit used in on-line editing.

Coincidental A method of checking the viewers of a program by phoning a sample of possible viewers while the program is in progress.

Commercial The advertiser's message on television or radio.

Concept The translation of a strategy into an idea that is the basis for a commercial.

Conform A final computer-controlled edit on 1-inch videotape that matches the off-line edit on videotape or film.

Continuity (1) Script for a television or radio program. (2) The flow or sequential development of a commercial.

Control room The room adjacent to the television studio or recording studio, from which the video and/or audio is coordinated.

Copywriter The person who, teamed with an art director, generates a concept for a commercial, and who writes the storyboard. In production, the copywriter works with the script supervisor to make sure the lines are covered, and with the director to make sure the interpretation of the lines is correct.

Cost per thousand The ratio of the cost of a television or radio advertisement (in dollars) to the number of households (in thousands) or to the number of individuals (in thousands) estimated to be in the audience at the time the advertisement is broadcast. The term is more fully referred to as "cost per thousand households (or homes)" or "cost per thousand viewers."

Coverage (1) The number of households or individuals, regardless of where located, that are able to receive a given television or radio station or group of stations. (2) How many ways a particular scene will be shot. While it is desirable to cover a scene many ways, such as CU, MS, dolly shot, and so on, coverage must always be a balance between having adequate material for editing versus the cost of film, the time budgeted for the shoot, and the fatigue level of the performers.

Cowcatcher An isolated commercial announcement at the beginning of a program that advertises a "secondary" product of the sponsor. This secondary product is not mentioned in the program itself.

Crab dolly Generally, a camera move in which the camera pans the subject while the dolly (the camera's moveable base) is being moved.

Crawl Graphics (usually credit copy) that move slowly up the screen; usually mounted on a drum that can also be called a "crawl."

Creative boutique An advertising agency that specializes in the creative product and does not offer full agency services, such as media, research, and so on.

Crew All the crafts people who work on a commercial.

Cue A signal given to an actor or to a member of the crew to do something at a certain time during a take.

Cross-fade In television, the fading out of one picture and the simultaneous fading in of another. In radio, the fading out of dialogue, sound, or music while simultaneously fading in other dialogue, sound, or music.

CU A close-up shot. Narrow angle picture. Usually a bust or head shot of a person or a full-screen image of an object.

Cue (1) The final words of an announcer's speech or actor's line used as a signal for another actor or announcer to begin. (2) A sound or musical effect. (3) A manual or audio signal from a director calling for action.

Cut (1) A signal to stop performers. (2) The deletion of program material to fit a pre-scribed period of time. (3) The simplest transition from one TV commercial scene to another in which the final frame of one scene changes abruptly to that of another scene.

Cut-in The insertion of a local announcement on cue into a network or transcribed program. Also termed a "cut-in announcement" or a "local cut-in."

Cut to (1) A fast switch from the picture on one camera to the picture on another. (2) An abrupt change of scene without a dissolve or wipe.

Cycle A certain amount of time a commercial may be aired without having to pay union talent an additional fee. A normal cycle is 13 weeks.

D-1, D-2, D-3, etc. Digital videotape formats.

Dead spot A section of audio track that sounds peculiar because it is absolutely quiet, instead of having a faint background ambience.

Demographic characteristics As used in broadcast research, a broad term that refers to the various social and economic characteristics of a group of households, or a group of individuals. For example, the term is used to refer to such characteristics as the number of members of a household, age of head of household, occupation of head of household, education of household members, and annual household income.

Depth of field The distance within which a subject can move toward or away from the camera without going out of focus, assuming no camera adjustment.

Diary method A panel method designed to study broadcast audiences for short periods of time, usually one week.

Digital Recording, whether audio or video, that reproduces the original as a series of numbers (digits) that can be understood and manipulated by a computer.

Diorama A miniature setting, complete in detail and perspective, used as a means of establishing large locations impossible to construct or restage in the studio.

Director (1) In TV and radio programming, the person responsible for the rehearsal and performance. (2) For commercials, the person who rehearses actors and announcers, guides camera operators, orders lighting effects, and works with the producer—in short, the person in charge on the set or location.

Director of photography The person responsible for the lighting during a shoot. Also called a cinematographer.

Direct response The business of selling products or services directly to the customer without the use of retail stores.

Dissolve (DS or DISS) (1) A combination fade-in and fade-out; a new scene appears while the preceding scene vanishes. When an object in the first scene apparently remains on screen for the second scene, it is called a "match dissolve." (2) Transitional device to indicate lapse of time by shifting the camera image slowly from one picture to another. (3) The overlapping fade-out of one picture and fade-in of another.

Dolly A moveable carriage usually mounted on four wheels that carries either a camera or a camera and camera operator.

Dolly camera A TV camera mounted on a small boom that is mounted on a four-wheel base. Has the advantage of greater height and mobility. It requires a special dolly pusher.

Dolly in To move in from a distance for a close-up by means of a camera mounted on a dolly.

Dolly out The reverse of *dolly in*. Also called "dolly back."

Double exposure To shoot a scene, rewind the camera, and shoot another scene on the same film. Literally, to expose the film twice, so that two images appear on the screen simultaneously, creating a particular effect.

Down and under A direction denoting that voices, music, and sound effects should now be heard at a lower level.

Drift To move the camera in or out on a scene almost imperceptibly.

Drop-in In broadcasting, a local commercial inserted in a nationally sponsored network program.

Dry runs Those rehearsals previous to camera rehearsals in which business, lines, sets, and so on are perfected.

Dubbing (1) Recording actor's and/or announcer's lip sync to film already shot. (2) Copying of an audio tape or a videotape.

ECU Abbreviation for extreme close-up. A shot showing only a portion of a face or other object. See *BCU, TCU.*

Edit To assemble the various scenes that were shot into a commercial.

Edit on disc To transfer takes from a film shoot onto video disc to do a rough cut.

Edit on film To select takes and do a rough cut on film.

Edit on tape To transfer takes from a film shoot onto videotape to do a rough cut.

Editor The person who edits a commercial and generally is responsible for postproduction.

Establishing shot A view of a scene wide and deep enough to establish the relationships of the people and objects in it.

EQ (Equalization) To set a standard level for all parts of an audio recording. To balance out the various frequencies of the recording.

Establishing shot A shot where the camera is as far away from the subject as possible while including everything that sets the scene.

Exterior (EXT) A scene filmed outside. See *interior.*

Extra A person, usually one of many, used in background shots, crowd shots, parties, and so on. Such persons have no lines and cannot be recognized.

Fade-in To gradually increase the intensity of a video picture from black to full scene.

Fade-out From full brightness, a picture gradually disappears until the screen is dark. The decreasing of signal strength.

Fast motion Action on film that appears faster than in real life. To achieve fast motion the camera is run at a slower speed than normal. See slow motion.

Fatigue The tendency of a commercial to lose its effectiveness over time.

Field A measurement of the area a scene occupies. A guide as to how much a scene may be enlarged.

Film-to-tape transfer To transcribe scenes of a commercial shot on film onto videotape.

Fixed focus The focus of the lens is not changed regardless of what movement takes place in front of the camera.

Flash cut To intersperse scenes of a second or less.

Flare A subject, usually metallic or glossy, that acts like a mirror, reflecting too much light. A flare most often occurs when the subject is moved.

Flat Lack of contrast in a screen image. Also, term for a scenic unit.

Floor manager The production person who heads the crew in a live television studio. Transmits the control director's instructions to actors and others on set.

"Following" shot The camera follows the movement of the subject without necessarily moving itself.

Frame In motion pictures, a single picture of the many that make up the whole. In television, the field of view in any particular shot. Adjustments in this are known as framing. An improper adjustment is off frame. When the subject crowds the sides of the picture, it is tight framing; when there is plenty of room, it is loose framing.

Frames per second (FPS) The number of individual pictures taken by a camera each second it is running. Normal speed in film is 24 frames per second, in video it is 30 frames per second.

Free-lance A self-employed person who works independently, not employed by an agency or company.

Freeze frame A film technique of holding a particular frame still on the screen for a desired time length. Often used at the close of a commercial.

Frequency The number of times a commercial airs each week.

Fringe time In television, the hours before or after prime viewing hours.

From the top An order to start rehearsal from the beginning of the musical number or script. May also refer to the start of a scene currently being rehearsed.

Full shot A full-length view of actors or talent.

Gaffer The person responsible for everything electrical on a shoot.

Generation In film or tape, relating to the distance a copy is away from the original. A master would be first generation; the first dub would be second generation; the second dub would be the third generation, and so on.

Go to black The picture is gradually faded out; same as *fade to black, fade-out.*

Golden time Whenever filming of a TV commercial runs overtime, the costs mount rapidly; this time is considered to be "golden."

Grip The general crew members available on a shoot for such odd jobs as moving or adjusting sets or repairing props.

Group shot A take that includes a number of people.

GRP (Gross rating points) A measure of the media weight supporting a given commercial. The GRP is the frequency multiplied by the reach (GRP = F × R).

Hair and makeup The person responsible for the actors' hairstyles and theatrical makeup on a shoot.

Hand-held To make a shot with the camera held in the hands. Also, a handle that can be mounted on a camera for this purpose.

Head The opening frames of a take, which may be used in their entirety or cut, to help achieve a smooth transition between scenes. See *tail.*

Head shot A close-up of an actor's or announcer's head, usually from the shoulders up.

Heavy-up To increase media spending.

Hidden camera A commercial technique in which a real person does not know he or she is being filmed.

Hiatus A break in the advertiser's broadcast schedule.

Hitchhike A short commercial tagged on the end of a program, advertising another product of the company sponsoring the program. When at the front, it is a "cowcatcher."

Hot (1) In audio, when a component on the mix, usually the music, is too loud in relation to the other components. (2) In video, when a certain part of a scene, or the entire scene, is too bright.

Hot set A set where nothing is to be touched or moved, to maintain continuity between days of shooting.

Hot spot A small area in a scene that is too bright.

I.D. Station identification; a 10-second spot on television used at station breaks. Time enough for the product name and claim—and a lot of creative ingenuity.

Image (1) In film, what the camera captures. (2) In advertising, the feelings in a person the product elicits, the emotional reasons to buy it, as opposed to the logical reasons for buying it. Also called *brand image*.

Impressions The number of times an individual sees a particular commercial.

Infomercial A long-form (28-minute) television commercial.

Integrated commercial A multiple-product TV commercial in which two or more products are presented within the framework of a single announcement.

Interior (INT) A scene filmed indoors. See *exterior*.

Interlock Any arrangement permitting the synchronous presentation of picture and matching sound from separate films. The simplest consists of a mechanical link connecting projector and sound reproducer, both being driven by a common synchronous drive.

In the can Scenes that have been shot but are not included in the final edited version of the commercial.

Jingle A song created to help sell a product or service.

Jump cut A scene that does not flow smoothly from the previous one, usually because the focus of attention shifts from one part of the frame to another. For example, if an actor is on the right of one scene and then appears on the left of the next.

Key lighting Pinpoint, intense light focused on a small area for highlight effect.

Lap dissolve Cross fading of one scene or image over another. Momentarily both pictures are visible. One picture disappears as another picture appears.

Leader (academy leader) The film that precedes the commercial opening. Usually 10 seconds. It has positioning and focus references to guide the video engineer, and numbers sequenced in seconds from nine down to three. Then the film is black for three seconds before the opening frame of the commercial.

"Limbo" shot Pictures taken against nonrecognized background. Often used with close-ups where background is nonessential.

Limited use A commercial that is only to run in certain areas or for a certain length of time.

Level The amount or quantity of loudness of sound. Also, level of light.

Lip-synchronization (lip-sync) Recording of a voice or voices to match the exact movement of actors' lips in a film already recorded. Or it can mean the filming of scenes with actors' lips moving to match a prerecorded track.

Live In television, a program or commercial that is being telecast as it originates.

Location The place or area away from a film studio in which a commercial or other part might be filmed.

Lock off A camera that does not move throughout a scene or an entire commercial.

Logotype (logo) The sponsor's or brand name's identifying signature or trademark.

Loop To combine a short section of video or audio track so that it repeats itself and appears to be longer.

LS Long shot. A full view of a set or background usually including a full-length view of actor or actors.

Make-good Credit for a missed commercial or program or a rebroadcast in a comparable time period to make up for one unavoidably cancelled, omitted, or not shown clearly or in its entirety.

Mandatories Anything that because of legal reasons or client dictates, must be included in a commercial.

Master The first-generation 1-inch videotape of a commercial with all the titles and supers. The master is usually duplicated for insurance against loss or damage and this second-generation tape is called a protection master. The master is then sent to a dubbing service to make multiple copies, which are sent to TV stations for airing.

Match dissolve   To end one scene with a similar scene, so that the images blend together and the audience is not immediately aware of the change.

Matting (matte)   A technique in which one part of a picture is photographed in one location and another in a different location, and then the two are combined in the printing process so that they appear to have been photographed at the same time and place.

Medium shot   Somewhere between a close-up and a long shot.

Mix   The sound studio session at which two or three or more sound tracks are combined.

Mix to pix   Fitting the audio of a commercial to the video, as opposed to fitting the video to the audio.

Mobile unit   Field equipment housed in special trucks for the televising or taping of an event remote from the studio.

Monitor   A control kinescope used by personnel (producer, switcher, technical director) to check and preview camera pickups or on-the-air pictures.

Montage   A sequence of short scenes that together convey an idea that could not be conveyed by any one of them alone. Sometimes several of the scenes appear on the screen at once; sometimes one blends into another; sometimes they appear in quick succession.

Morphing   A commercial technique that digitally transforms one object into another.

Mortise   A small section of a scene that shows another scene. Often used to show a product shot in a live action scene or a close-up of a face in a product shot.

MOS   A portion of a film without sound, with wild sound added later. See *sync sound.*

Moving shot   Any scene where the camera physically moves.

Move in   A storyboard designation describing camera movement toward the subject being photographed. Also "zoom in."

MS   Abbreviation for medium shot. Somewhere between a close-up (CU) and a long shot (LS).

MS and MCU   Medium shot and medium close-up. Camera instructions indicating that the subject should be seen in relation to some but not all other elements in a scene, the latter being more restrictive than the former.

Multiple exposure   Various pictures appearing in one scene.

Multi track   In audio, the process and equipment used for recording and/or mixing where different voices, instruments, and so on, have their own discrete sound track. Depending on the complexity of the project, as many as 64 tracks may be used.

Narrator   An off-camera or background voice. Refers also to an on-camera spokesperson relating the story line of a script.

Network   Interconnecting broadcasting stations for the simultaneous broadcasting of TV or radio programs.

Nonlinear random access   Editing on a computer. This allows for instant access to any place in the commercial, compared to real-time editing on film or videotape.

No seam   Fabric or paper on a roll that can be pulled down and toward the camera, like a window shade, and create a surface with no horizon line or angles. A surface on which a subject may be shot. See *sweep.*

NTI   Nielsen Television Index. A limited but projectable rating system that helps determine a TV program's viewing audience.

Off camera   An actor or announcer's voice that is heard although the actor or announcer does not appear on screen.

Off line   Rough editing that is usually done in an editing suite with limited equipment and at less cost than final editing, which is done on 1-inch videotape and on an on-line editing system.

Off-screen narration   Any narration that is not lipsync. Also referred to as "voice-over."

On-camera   (1) An actor or announcer delivers lines as he or she appears on the screen. (2) Whatever is included within the scope of the lens.

On-line   Final editing that is done on 1-inch videotape in a state-of-the-art, expensive editing suite. On line means that the equipment is controlled by computers.

Opaques Non-transparent artwork or visuals (for example, a photo, postcard, or picture from a magazine). Variations: (1) "Flip": opaque artwork or titles mounted on a heavy card, flipped vertically or horizontally. (2) Draw cards: some material pulled manually or mechanically from its position, either horizontally, vertically, or obliquely.

Open end (1) A broadcast in which the commercial spots are added locally. (2) A network commercial complete except for the final seconds of audio or video that are cut in locally.

Optical Special photographic effects, such as the dissolving of one scene into another, wiping out of one scene and appearance of another (wipe), a motion picture within the film, (matte shot), grouping of several scenes simultaneously (montage), and so on.

Optical view finder The device on a camera used by the cameraman to accurately frame and focus the scene to be televised or filmed.

Out of synch A scene in which the spoken words do not match up to the lip movement. The audio is either starting or ending at a different time than the video.

Outs Takes or portions of takes that have been discarded.

Outtake A take that is not used in the final edit.

Over crank To operate a camera at a faster-than-normal speed, which makes the action appear to move slower than normal. See *Under crank.*

Over scale A rate of pay that is more than the standard rate of pay for a particular job. Star personalities often demand, and receive, over-scale compensation.

Over-the-shoulder shot A camera shot of a performer from across the shoulder of the character to whom he is speaking.

PA (Production assistant) A person learning the production business, and who runs general errands on a shoot.

Paintbox The brand name of an electronic special effects device that lets the user "paint" a scene on film.

Pan An abbreviation of panoramic. To "pan" is to move the camera, either left or right, without moving the dolly or base. A movement up or down is properly called a "tilt," but on some scripts you sill see the direction "pan up" instead of "tilt up."

Parity claim An advertising statement that, because of clever wording, seems to say the product is superior to the competition, but in reality only says no other product is better. For example, the Quaker Oats slogan, "Nothing is better for thee than me," leaves open the possibility that other cereals may be as nutritious as Quaker Oats. Or, "Nothing outlasts the Energizer," which tries to deal with the fact that battery technology is the same among brands.

Participating program A TV or radio show in which a number of advertisers have their products featured or mentioned.

Pedestal camera A TV camera mounted on a pneumatically controlled base allowing for greater movement in the studio. Must be moved by a cameraperson or operator.

Picture resolution The clarity with which the TV image appears on the TV screen.

Piggyback A one-minute time segment in which a sponsor can show two commercials, each featuring a different product.

Playback The replaying of a tape for review and correction purposes.

Positioning In advertising, the place the product or service occupies in the consumer's mind, compared to other products or services in the category.

Positive A projection print from negative film. The true picture.

Postproduction Everything related to producing a commercial that takes place after the shooting.

Preempt Telecasting time made available for a special event, which takes the place of the regularly scheduled program.

Preproduction Everything related to producing a commercial that takes place before shooting.

Prime time A continuous period of not less than three hours of the broadcast day during which the station's audience is the greatest. In television, usually from 7:00 to 11:00 p.m. in the East and from 6:00 to 10:00 p.m. in the Midwest and West.

Principal An on-camera actor who performs in a commercial. If a SAG or AFTRA player says one word of dialogue and/or can be recognized in one scene, he or she is considered a principal and must be paid accordingly.

Prism lens A special lens with several facets that breaks one picture up into many. Used for special effects—as when multiple images of a dancer are seen on many parts of the screen.

Process shot A shot involving an unusual process of some sort, especially rear projection (either still or in motion), with the live action taking place in front of the projected picture; shooting through glass on which scenes are painted, with live action taking place behind it; or the use of miniature sets combined with live action in such a way as to create the impression of reality.

Producer The coordinator and overseer of all aspects of getting a TV storyboard onto film or tape. Responsible for budget, schedules, talent, and meeting deadlines.

Production values The aesthetics of a commercial, which are influenced by the quality of the actors' performances, the directing, lighting, editing, music, and so on, as well as by the quality of the original stock, the props, sets, studios, equipment, and so on.

Product protection In television, the assurance to an advertiser of a time lapse between his commercial and that of a competitor. Given by a station or network, such protection assurance is usually up to 15 minutes.

Promo Spot ad plugging a program, station, or service.

Props From "properties." All the articles in a production that are the property of the producing company or are rented by the company; notably furnishings and decorations, but including an infinite variety of items, large and small, from ashtrays to zircons.

Psychographics The goals, values, ambitions, and beliefs of a group of consumers.

Pull-back A storyboard designation describing camera movement away from the subject being photographed. (Also zoom-back, move-back.)

Quick cut A change of scene of short duration.

Rack focus A scene where the camera quickly changes focus from the foreground to the background, or vice versa.

Rate card A chart that lists the cost of broadcast time on a station based on the length of the announcement and the number of times it is used on the air.

Rating The percentage of a statistical sample of families who have a radio and/or television set available and who reported hearing or viewing a particular program when interviewed.

Rating points In broadcast, the percentage of potential audience tuned to a specific station for a specific program.

Reach The number of people who watch a TV station at any given time of day.

Real person An ordinary person, not an actor or a celebrity presenter, who testifies positively about a product or service in a commercial.

Rear projection A device that allows actors to be filmed in front of a screen on which is projected—from behind—a special background. A substitute for expensive location shooting. A device that allows an actor or announcer to be on camera while the background can be anything you want.

Remote A telecast originated outside the studio.

Reportage The style of shooting film with a hand-held camera, available light, and candidness. A cinema vérité technique that gives the film added realism, an unrehearsed quality.

Residuals Payments made to union talent every time a commercial runs.

Reveal To move the camera in a way that shows someone or something that was in the scene all the time.

Ripple dissolve A wave-like transition between scenes, usually done to convey a dream sequence or the passage of time.

Rollout To go from a test of a successful commercial to broadcasting on a large scale.

Room tone The natural ambient sound in a studio or location.

Rough cut The first crude assembly of a commercial without dissolves, effects, a mixed track, titles, supers, and so on.

Run-through   A rehearsal.

SAG   Screen Actors Guild. The union of performers in films who work for established scales of pay. The only time you may use a player who is not a member of SAG is when you are showing actual jobs or activities that non-SAG people alone are qualified to do. See *AFTRA*.

Saturation   A media term denoting high frequency of advertising impressions during a concentrated period of time.

Scale   The standard, established rates of pay for members of film and television unions.

Scene   A completed piece of action or dialogue. Usually all the action and dialogue taking place continuously with the same background. Also, a setting or location for action.

Scratch track   A rough recording of the audio track, usually done by the producer, on the rough cut. The search track has no music or sound effects and is not mixed.

Script   The commercial, written as a manuscript or in screenplay form. See *storyboard*.

Script notes   A written record of each take, indicating its number, its length, and if there was anything particularly good or bad about it.

Script supervisor   The person responsible for keeping script notes, checking the length and accuracy of takes, and maintaining continuity during shooting.

Segue   In music, the bridge or transition from one theme to another.

Selects   Takes that have been printed or takes that have been chosen.

Set   A TV scene used or constructed in the studio in which action takes place and is filmed.

Set designer   A person who creates a set and furnishes it with props.

Share of audience   Generally, the percentage of the aggregate television or radio audience in some specified area of a given network, station, or program. Frequently referred to simply as "share."

Shock cut   Sudden, abrupt cut to a particular dramatic scene or action.

Shooting date   The day designated for the start of actual filming.

Shooting schedule   The order in which scenes will be filmed during a shooting day. If the scenes are to be shot in the order in which they will appear on film, the shooting is in sequence. If the scenes are not to be shot in the order in which they will appear on film, which is the usual case, the shooting is out of sequence.

Signatory   A company or individual that has signed the SAG and/or AFTRA contracts, which means agreeing to only use SAG and AFTRA talent in commercial production.

Signature   The name and/or logo or trademark of the advertiser.

Simulcast   The simultaneous playing of a program over television and radio. (Also, a stereo broadcast over two radio stations.)

Slate   (1) A board on which is written the title of the production, the director, the cameraperson, the scene number, and the take number. The slate is held in front of the camera before each take. (2) An electronic device that records the scene, take number, and frame. (3) A notice that comes on screen before a commercial, listing the client, commercial name, commercial number, advertising agency, production company, producer, and date.

Slide   A title or picture on a single frame of 35mm film that is projected into the camera. Called "transparencies," they are invariably glass mounted. (May be other than 35mm in size.)

Slow motion   Action on film or video that appears slower than real life. To achieve slow motion the camera is run faster than normal. See *fast motion*.

Slug   A piece of film, usually white leader, put in the place where a scene will eventually go.

Small speaker   A speaker used in a recording studio that approximates the relatively low-fidelity, monaural speaker in a normal TV set, as opposed to the high-fidelity, stereo speakers used for mixing. The small speaker is used to hear what the mix will sound like in "real life."

Smoke   A harmless chemical used to fog up a scene, softening the light and creating a particular mood and feeling.

SMPTE   (Society of Motion Picture and Television Engineers) The association of professionals who set the engineering and technical standards for all aspects of film and video production and transmission.

Sneak   To bring in a sound or a music cue at low volume without distracting the attention of the listener. After an effect has served its purpose, it may be "sneaked out" in like manner.

SOF   Sound on film.

Soft cut   A transition between scenes that is quicker than a cut but slower than a dissolve.

Soft focus   To throw a scene slightly out of focus, thus softening its look.

Sound effects (SFX)   Various devices or recordings used to simulate lifelike sounds. On storyboards, the abbreviation SFX is used before indicating the sound effect desired.

Soundstage   A stage that is soundproofed, so that on-camera sound may be recorded there.

Spec sheet   A list of specifications about a product or advertiser, to be included in a commercial by an announcer who creates his or her own wording for the commercial. (Also called a fact sheet.)

Special effects   Miniatures, diorama, or various electrical, film, or mechanical devices used to simulate impressive backgrounds, massive titles, and so on. Any device used to achieve scenic or dramatic effects impossible in actual or full-scale production in the TV studio.

Splice   To join together two pieces of film with film cement.

Split screen   A special effect utilizing two or more cameras so that two or more screens are visible simultaneously on separate parts of the screen (for example, two people holding a telephone conversation).

Sponsor   The firm or individual that pays for broadcast time and talent.

Spot   (1) Spotlight. (2) Time segment of one minute or less sold by stations for advertisements.

Spot commercial   Commercial of one minute or less, usually on film or tape. It may be shown within a program or adjacent to it.

Spot television   Generally, commercial messages within shows not totally sponsored by one firm or commercials shown during station breaks, as opposed to commercials within the framework of one sponsor's program. Also, the spotting of commercials in selected geographical locations.

Sound track   The recorded audio portion of a filmed or taped commercial.

Station break   A brief break in the programming so that a station may identify itself. An "hour" network program actually runs only 59 minutes and 25 seconds, the next five seconds being used for network identification, the following 20 for a commercial, and the final 10 for another commercial including two seconds for local station identification. A half-hour network program runs 29 minutes and 25 seconds.

Steadicam   The brand name of a counterbalanced mount for hand-held cameras that helps to smooth out and steady the camera as it is moved.

Still   A still photograph or other illustrative material that may be used in a TV broadcast.

Stock shot   A scene not filmed especially for the production, but taken from film files or a film library.

Stop motion   Film taken by exposing one frame instead of many frames at a time. An object or objects are usually moved a fraction of an inch for each exposure according to a predetermined pattern.

Storyboard   Drawings or photographs arranged in sequence that show the visual continuity of a commercial, with copy adjacent to each picture describing the video action and the audio portion.

Strategy   The main argument(s) for buying a product or service. Sometimes called communication strategy or creative strategy. See *image*, *positioning*, and *USP*.

Strike   To undo a setup after it has been shot. To physically disassemble a set.

Studio   (1) At a TV station, a room from which programs emanate. (2) At a film production house, the room in which commercials are filmed.

Super   Abbreviation for *superimposition*. One picture (usually opaque titles) is imposed in front of another picture, and both are seen simultaneously.

Sweep   The floor of a set, whether tabletop or a stage, that curves upward toward the background and flows into the rear wall so that no horizon line can be seen. See *no seam.*

Sync   Synchronization; the simultaneous projection of picture and sound; also, the electronic pulses of picture transmitter and receiver must be synchronized to produce a stable image on the television screen.

Tabletop   Any small-scale production that uses small props and no on-camera actors.

Tag   An addition to a commercial, announcement, or musical gimmick that acts as a finale to that segment.

Tail   The closing frames of a take, which may be used in their entirety or cut to help achieve a smooth transition between scenes. See *head.*

Take   (1) Switching directly from one picture or camera to another picture or camera, as "take one, take two," (2) Individual filmed or taped sequences or scenes.

Talent   An all-inclusive word referring to actors, announcers, musicians, or performers.

TCU   Tight close-up; narrow angle picture. See also: *BCU, ECU.*

Technical director   The director of all camera or video facilities from a television station.

Telephoto lens   A very narrow angle lens that produces large images at extreme distance; frequently used at sporting events, and so on.

TelePrompTer   A patented machine on which a large version of the script can be unrolled at any desired speed, operated out of camera range to prompt actors; usually mounted on the camera near the lens turret. The reader appears to look almost directly at the viewer when using a TelPrompTer on live camera.

Televise   To transmit a picture electronically using TV equipment.

Telop   An opaque photograph or drawing projected by the telop projector.

Tight shot   A picture that fills the screen with a single object of interest so that no background detail distracts from it.

Tilt   A camera movement, pivoting on the horizontal axis, up or down.

Tilt-up   A storyboard designation describing an upward pan of the camera. (Tilt-down is the reverse movement.)

Time lapse   A type of filming in which individual frames are shot at relatively long intervals. This technique compress time events of long duration, such as the opening of a flower, into a few seconds.

Title camera   A camera mounted on a frame so that it faces down and can be moved. Below it is a flat bed on which items to be filmed are placed. A title camera is ordinarily used for flat art, supers, and 800 numbers that have been set as typography.

Titles   Any title used on a TV program or commercial. Can be motion picture film, cards, slides, and so on.

Track   (1) In audio, the sound portion of a film or video. Any discrete recording of the audio track, such as the voice track, the music track, the sound effects track. (2) Any subdivision of the music track: for example, the guitar track, the drum track, and so on. (3) In shooting, parallel rails along which a dolly travels during a moving shot.

Transparency   A technique whereby illustrative or written material is placed on a transparent surface through which background material may be seen as the transparency is picked up by the TV camera.

Trim   Any part of a take that is discarded. See *head* and *tail.*

Truck   A movement of a studio camera, left or right, parallel to the plane of action.

Trucking   The camera moving beside a character or object that is in motion.

Truck shot   A camera, mounted on a moveable dolly, is guided along a certain prescribed path marked on the studio floor. This gives an effect of moving toward, past, or away from whatever is to be filmed.

TVB   Television Bureau of Advertising.

Two shot   Often printed "2-shot"; refers to a picture in which two persons are seen. ("3-shot" includes three people.)

U-Matic   The brand name of ¾-inch videotape, players, and recorders.

Under crank   To operate a camera at a slower-than-normal speed, which makes the action appear to move faster than normal. See *Over crank*.

Union talent   Actors and actresses that belong to AFTRA and/or SAG. Most belong to both.

USP (unique selling proposition)   An advertising philosophy developed in the 1950s by Rosser Reeves for Ted Bates & Company. A good USP tells the customer something that makes him or her want to buy the product and that is, or seems to be, an exclusive feature of the product.

Vampire video   A commercial in which some aspect of the production is so interesting and entertaining that viewers forget who the advertiser is.

Viewfinder   A small television set on top of the camera in which the camera operator sees the picture being photographed.

Viewing lens   The lens on a TV camera used by the camera operator to view the field of action.

Video   The visual, pictorial portion of a television program, announcement, or commercial.

Video disc   An editing format that uses laser disc technology similar to a home CD.

Videotape recording   An electronic system that permits the recording of video and audio on a continuous strip of tape. It requires no laboratory processing, can be rewound and played back immediately. and can be edited immediately after recording. Film is transferred to videotape for use in telecasting.

Visual time code   A series of numbers that have been superimposed on videotape to help an editor locate scenes and frames within them.

Voice-over (VO)   In television, a commercial, film, or live sequence in which an actor's or announcer's voice is heard, but the person is not seen.

Wardrobe   The clothes worn by an actor.

Wardrobe supervisor   The person responsible for selecting, acquiring, and fitting clothing or costumes for actors in a commercial.

Whip shot   A fast pan shot, blurring the action on the screen.

Whiz pan   A camera swung very rapidly left to right or right to left, blurring the scene. Used as a dramatic device to shift from one scene to another or one object of interest to another, or for comic effects, simulating a double take. Also known as a blur pan, swish pan, and whip shot.

Wide-angle lens   A special lens that permits a greater view of the field, left and right.

Wide-angle shot   A shot that makes it possible for the camera to cut a wide scene from a shallow depth.

Wide shot   A shot that covers a large area.

Wild sound   Sound that is recorded without being in sync with the picture. See *sync sound*.

Wipe   An optical effect in which a line or object appears to move across the screen revealing a new picture. A wipe may stop midway and become a split-screen effect.

Wipe over   Optical film or printing effect by which one scene or image moves into another geometrically.

Wrap   The end of shooting, either for the day or for the production. The wrap often happens in stages. For example, if the live action is finished but the product shots remain, the director will say: "Wrap talent, sound, hair and makeup, and wardrobe."

XCU   Extreme close-up; same as ECU.

Zoom   The change in focal length of a special lens (Zoomar lens) that gives the effect of moving either toward or away from an object.

Zoomar   An adjustable lens that can zoom from a focal length of one size to another without loss of focus or light.

Zoom lens   A special lens on a motion picture and TV camera that permits slow rapid movement either toward or away from the photographed subject. Can be used in studios or on location. Can be used to cover a great distance quickly.

Bibliography

Baldwin, Hintley. *Creating Effective TV Commercials.* Lincolnwood, IL: NTC Business Books, 1982.

Belch, George E., and Michael A. Belch. *Introduction to Advertising and Promotion,* 2nd ed. Burr Ridge, IL: Richard D. Irwin, Inc., 1993.

Bellaire, Arthur. *The Bellaire Guide to TV Commercial Cost Control.* Lincolnwood, IL: NTC Business Books, 1982.

Book, Albert C., and C. Dennis Schick. *Fundamentals of Copy and Layout.* Lincolnwood, IL: NTC Business Books, 1984.

Bovee, Courtland L., and William F. Arens. *Contemporary Advertising.* Homewood, IL: Richard D. Irwin, 1983.

Brady, Frank R., and Vasquez, J. Angel. *Direct Response Television: The Authoritative Guide.* Lincolnwood, IL: NTC Business Books, 1995.

Busch, H. Ted, and Terry Landeck. *The Making of a Television Commercial.* New York, NY: Macmillan Publishing Co., Inc., 1980.

Diamant, Lincoln. *Dictionary of Broadcast Communications.* 3rd ed. Lincolnwood, IL: NTC Business Books, 1991.

Eicoff, Al. *Direct Marketing Through Broadcast Media.* Lincolnwood, IL: NTC Business Books, 1995.

Heighton, Elizabeth, and Don R. Cunningham. *Advertising in the Broadcast Media.* Belmont, CA: Wadsworth Publishing Co., 1980.

Hopkins, Claude. *Scientific Advertising.* Lincolnwood, IL: NTC Business Books, 1995.

Katz, Helen. *The Media Handbook: A Complete Guide to Advertising Media Selection, Planning, Research & Buying.* Lincolnwood, IL: NTC Business Books, 1995.

Mandell, Maurice I. *Advertising.* 3rd ed. Englewood Cliffs, NJ: Prentice-Hall, 1980.

Ogilvy, David. *Ogilvy on Advertising.* New York, NY: Vintage Books, 1985.

Reeves, Rosser. *Reality in Advertising.* New York, NY: Alfred A. Knopf, 1986.

Ries, Al, and Jack Trout. *Positioning.* New York, NY: McGraw-Hill, 1986.

Sandage, Charles H., et al. *Advertising: Theory and Practice.* 11th ed. Homewood, IL: Richard D. Irwin, 1983.

Schulberg, Peter. *Radio Advertising: The Authoritative Handbook.* Lincolnwood, IL: NTC Business Books, 1996.

White, Hooper. *How to Produce an Effective TV Commercial.* Lincolnwood, IL: NTC Business Books, 1994.

Wright, John S., et. al. *Advertising.* 5th ed. New York, NY: McGraw-Hill, 1982.

Young, James Webb. *A Technique for Producing Ideas.* Lincolnwood, IL: NTC Business Books, 1975.

Zeigler, Sherilyn K., and Herbert H. Howard. *Broadcast Advertising.* 2nd ed. Columbus, OH: Grid Publishing Co., 1983.